THE STRAY BULLET

TRANSLATED BY DANIEL C. SCHECHTER

UNIVERSITY OF MINNESOTA PRESS

MINNEAPOLIS • LONDON

WILLIAM S.

BURROUGHS

IN MEXICO

JORGE GARCÍA-ROBLES

Originally published in Spanish as *La bala perdida: William S. Burroughs en México, 1949–1952* (Mexico City: Ediciones del Milenio, 1995) and later republished in *Burroughs y Kerouac: Dos forasteros perdidos en México* (Mexico City: Random House Mondadori, 2007). Copyright 2006 Jorge García-Robles. Copyright 2007 Random House Mondadori, S. A. de C. V.

English translation copyright 2013 by the Regents of the University of Minnesota

Published by the University of Minnesota Press
111 Third Avenue South, Suite 290
Minneapolis, MN 55401-2520
http://www.upress.umn.edu

Library of Congress Cataloging-in-Publication Data
    García-Robles, Jorge, 1956–
    [Bala perdida. English]
    The stray bullet : William S. Burroughs in Mexico / Jorge García-Robles ; translated by Daniel C. Schechter.
    Includes bibliographical references.
    ISBN 978-0-8166-8062-7 (hc)
    ISBN 978-0-8166-8063-4 (pb)
    1. Burroughs, William S., 1914–1997—Homes and haunts—Mexico. 2. Novelists, American—20th century—Biography. 3. Fugitives from justice—Mexico—Biography. 4. Mexico—Intellectual life—20th century. 5. Americans—Mexico—Biography. I. Schechter, Daniel C., translator. II. Title.
PS3552.U75Z6813 2013
813'.54—dc23
[B]   2013018887

Printed in the United States of America on acid-free paper

The University of Minnesota is an equal-opportunity educator and employer.

20 19 18 17 16 15 14 13   10 9 8 7 6 5 4 3 2 1

CONTENTS

PREFACE TO THE U.S. EDITION

For the majority of young Latin Americans in the 1970s, it was practically obligatory to unfurl the socialist banner and patently reject youth culture in all its forms, including rock, illicit drugs, Oriental religious traditions, and even the reading of certain writers considered outside the revolutionary agenda. Listening to Pink Floyd, smoking pot, attending a Hatha Yoga session, or reading Dostoyevsky were to be done on the sly, or at best on the margins of the rigorous canons of Marxism. In short, young people of that period were torn between their doctrinaire duties and their generational desires.

I was one of those who read novelists and poets that had nothing to do with the class struggle, from Melville and Stendhal to Artaud and Céline, making me the target of numerous critics who pegged me as petit bourgeois. By the time I was twenty-two, I had figured out that life was not as simple as Marxist liturgy had made it out to be, and I completely withdrew from its fundamentalist fantasies.

Socialism ceded to sixties counterculture, and therein sprang my interest in the Beat Generation. The counterculture struck me as a far more colorful universe, suitable for a young rebel, and reading the novels of Kerouac and Burroughs and the poetry of Ginsberg and Corso reinforced this belief. The Beats became my essential references for interpreting and evaluating the world around me.

Time passed, I ceased to be young, I published a couple of books, and I started teaching literature at the political science department of the National Autonomous University of Mexico (UNAM). When I was put in charge of cultural programs at the university, the first thing I did was to send a letter to William S. Burroughs inviting him to lead a conference. That was in 1989, and my interest in Burroughs and the Beats had remained strong. Burroughs (via his agent) responded that he couldn't go to Mexico—he no longer traveled by plane. Capitalizing on the connection, I requested a meeting with the author of *Naked Lunch*, and in August 1990 I caught a plane to Dallas, Texas, then a bus to Lawrence, Kansas. There, amid the drinks, clouds of marijuana smoke, and target practice, I made my first acquaintance with William Burroughs.

The meeting was contradictory. At first the idealized image I'd had of my hero brushed up against the reality: I was meeting a person of flesh and blood, with imperfections like the rest of us. Later, over time, I discovered the individual, the rara avis, someone who was not perfect but special and distinct.

Out of this journey came the idea of writing a book on Burroughs's stay in Mexico. I initially embarked on the project with James Grauerholz, the literary agent of the author of *Junky*, but James dropped out soon after, and I chose to continue alone. I threw myself into the project and investigated anything to do with the subject: I went to the periodicals library, I interviewed people who had known Burroughs forty years earlier and others who had known Lola la Chata and Bernabé Jurado, I scoured used bookstores for books and magazines, I read everything that Kerouac, Ginsberg, Corso, and others had written about Mexico, I researched the historical origins of the Roma district (where William and Joan Burroughs lived), and finally I finished the book, which was first published in Spanish in 1995.

While I was writing the book, my relationship with Burroughs developed in different ways. On one occasion while I was in Lawrence, Kansas, I asked him questions related to his time in Mexico and I realized he was avoiding the subject, especially when it came to personal matters; needless to say, I never got a word out of him on the death of Joan Vollmer.

Nevertheless, when I asked him to write on the Mexican lawyer Bernabé Jurado for the book, he agreed and drafted a piece on small index cards that he titled "My Most Unforgettable Character." It's in the book. Around that time, I sent him photographs of Mexico City during the period he had lived there. He had never seen them before. One was of Lola la Chata, the reigning queen of the Mexican drug trade in those years; he later used it in a series of paintings that were subsequently exhibited in several countries.

In January 1996, *La bala perdida* was presented in Mexico City, with the proceedings broadcast on a culturally oriented TV channel. Nearly a thousand people attended, much to the surprise of both myself and the organizers of the event. At one point, Burroughs spoke live from Lawrence via telephone and read his piece on Bernabé Jurado, concluding his participation with the celebrated words "¡Vámonos cabrones!" The presentation, press coverage, and various editions of the book published by Ediciones del Milenio and Random House (in 2008 a Swedish edition appeared) demonstrated that there was and is a significant sector of the public, most of them young, interested in the work and the figure of Burroughs and the Beats. I must admit that when I wrote the book, I was unaware of the size of that group.

The publication of a U.S. edition of *The Stray Bullet* seems as desirable as it is necessary. Unlikely as it appears, Burroughs is linked in many ways to American culture and civilization, even if he has been one of the country's harshest critics. It was the same with Aldous Huxley and D. H. Lawrence, who, although they said they hated England, remained as English as roast beef. American audiences are due a book that tells of the experiences one of its writers had in Mexico in the years 1949 to 1952, above all because those experiences were crucial to his personal and literary life, and ultimately because these experiences form part of American literary history.

Burroughs experienced Mexico in different ways: he celebrated it, detested it, enjoyed it, suffered it. In his own words, it was on Mexican soil that his fatal vocation as a writer was born. To explore the Mexico–Burroughs connection, to break it down, look into its nooks and crannies, study and exhibit its details—this was my original intent in writing this book. It's up to American readers to decide how well I have achieved it.

J. G.-R. Mexico City, 2012

PART I

THE ROAD
TO HELL

BLAME IT ON BRAHMS

Late 1943. World War II. New York. 15 degrees. The atomic bomb looms over the world. William Seward Burroughs moves invisibly through the Manhattan streets. He wears a Chesterfield coat. A bowler hat. A company of demons hover around him. Just back from Chicago, Burroughs has a friend in New York: Lucien Carr, a young Columbia student. One day Lucien was listening to Brahms's Trio No. 1 when he heard a slight knocking at the door. He turned the doorknob, opened the door, and saw a flustered young Jew of seventeen, with curly black hair and ridiculously thick glasses. What the fuck do you want? is not what he said but was about to. The young man wanted to know who composed the trio. Lucien invited him in, observed his visitor's face. Oh, he looks like Rimbaud, he thought with delight. They became friends. Allen Ginsberg.

Carr introduced Ginsberg to Burroughs, and Allen was amazed to hear him quote from Shakespeare to comment on a spat between lesbians at a bar. With him was David

Kamerer, a gay redhead, obsessively in love with Carr, who was not gay and had a friend along: Edie Parker. She in turn had a boyfriend then plying the Atlantic Ocean on a boat full of bombs and cannons, Jack Kerouac, and a girlfriend, Joan Vollmer Adams, with whom she shared an apartment on 118th Street. Back from the sea, Kerouac met Lucien and Ginsberg at Joan and Edie's place. One day Burroughs, who wanted to go to sea, went looking for Jack at Lucien's suggestion. When he got to his apartment he knocked on the door. Upon seeing Burroughs, Jack thought he looked "like a shy bank clerk with a patrician thinlipped cold bluelipped face, blue eyes saying nothing behind steel rims and glass."

Joan Vollmer was born in Loudonville, near Albany. She was twenty years old and had an infant, Julie, a husband, and various lovers, some of them younger than she was. The husband, stationed in Tennessee, wasn't sure if he was Julie's father. Joan studied journalism at Columbia; read and discussed Kant, Plato, and Proust at the West End, a bar near the university. Like Edie Parker, Joan jumped from bed to bed, from stud to stud, abortion to abortion, drank and took drugs.

Burroughs became shaman to Kerouac and Ginsberg. He had them read Spengler, Céline, Korzybski, Cocteau, Rimbaud, Hart Crane, Kafka . . . or he would sit them down on a couch to psychoanalyze them. Ginsberg would pour out his pain and shout out that nobody loved him. Sympathetically, WSB heard him out without saying a word, letting him vomit out everything he held inside.

Burroughs had received a degree in English literature from Harvard, without giving it too much importance. His academic and social status meant nothing to him. His family continued to send him two hundred dollars per month. In 1944 he turned thirty. He sometimes worked: in New York as a bartender, in Chicago as an exterminator. He studied medicine in Vienna for nine months but never visited Robert Musil. In Paris he never sought out the surrealists, nor André Gide, Joyce, Ezra Pound, Georges Bataille, Nikolai Berdyaev, Chagall, Picasso, or Sartre. In Athens he married a Jewess from Hamburg who lived in Dubrovnik and wore a monocle—Ilse Klapper—to get her out of Europe so the Nazis would not incinerate her. In 1943 he met Truman Capote in New York. To him, the writer seemed like a shriveled-up, aging albino with a shrill voice. Life bored him. He had read and thought and felt and always lived in a box seat in the human stadium, on the wrong side of life, on the other side of the world. And while he was teaching his charges how to loosen life's rusty bolts, he voluntarily got lost in the junkyards of his own soul.

On the morning of August 14, 1944, Lucien Carr, fed up with David Kamerer's annoying behavior, stabbed him to death in Morningside Park; he dragged the body to the Hudson, then ran over to Burroughs's house to tell him everything. Later he went to 118th Street looking for Kerouac. The two men went to the scene of the crime to remove the evidence. Later they went into a movie house to try and forget the matter. But two days later Lucien turned himself in to the police. It was a front-page story in the *New York Times*. The police arrested Burroughs and Kerouac for covering up. Mortimer Burroughs, William's father, flew from Saint Louis to New York with a $2,500 bail bond so they wouldn't lock up his defenseless son. In contrast, Kerouac's father said no, he couldn't help him out, saying his son had besmirched the family's reputation, an unforgivable sin. Lucien was sentenced to twenty years in prison but got out after two. Six days after the incident, Kerouac married Edie Parker, who paid his bail, using the marriage as a pretext not to go back to jail. The marriage lasted a few months. The stabbing also motivated Burroughs, who still wasn't sure about his vocation as a writer, and Kerouac, who was, to write a divertimento of a novel inspired by the affair, titled *And the Hippos Boiled in Their Tanks*.

WELCOME TO YOUR DESTINY

In 1945 Joan and Edie moved to an apartment at 419 West 115th Street. Edie worked as a cigarette girl at the Zanzibar nightclub. Kerouac, who had left her not long before, went back to live with them. Allen Ginsberg and Hal Chase (an anthropologist from Denver who at age sixteen had written an imaginary dialogue between Nietzsche and Dostoyevsky) also went to live on 115th Street. It was at that time that Joan Vollmer and William S. Burroughs had their first meeting, an encounter that was very carefully planned by Kerouac and Ginsberg, who rightly intuited they'd be compatible. From the start the two were attracted to each other, but time had to pass for the relationship to become conspiratorial and close. Other than that, the apartment on 115th Street lacked just one thing: for his highness Burroughs to move in, which he did before long.

A few months after the atomic bomb was dropped on Hiroshima, William S. Burroughs, who had been living alone in a small apartment on Bedford Street in Greenwich Village, packed his meager belongings, stealthily and imperceptibly crossed Manhattan, arrived at the apartment on 115th Street, and, leaving his bag on the ground, knocked on the door. It opened to reveal the fine silhouette of Joan, who in a soft voice said to him, "Welcome to your destiny." Burroughs responded, "Welcome to yours," then got his things and closed the door.

The Burroughs–Joan relationship, as bizarre and unusual as any recorded in twentieth-century literature, was odd from the outset. The two wanted to distance themselves from humanity; they never felt any guilt for their actions. They were the king and queen of 115th Street, reigning over the most brilliant souls of the American underground. Each dwelled in a separate universe, a centrifuge of human habits. Their coexistence remained outside every norm of conventional marriage. Burroughs never hid his homosexual tendencies; Joan did not disguise her somewhat libertine predilections. The two were prone to consuming alcohol and other substances, to respect nothing more than their own desires. Being so similar, they sometimes clashed. Joan in particular liked to provoke and sometimes attack Bill, who wasn't always able to rein her in. She told everyone, for example, how making love to him sometimes gave her foot cramps.

It was easier to comprehend Joan's reasons than Burroughs's for entering into this relationship. Her intelligence and grace coexisted with her inability to put down roots. Her soul was as lucid as it was incapable of living in this world. Joan was ruled by a powerful vocation for chaos and self-destruction. And this vocation was reaffirmed and channeled by Burroughs. It's why she joined him. Not to start a family nor to establish a secure bond that would protect her from the world; not to share her body, her mind, or her dreams with him, but to do exactly the opposite. But why did William S. Burroughs accept Joan? Why did Burroughs, an utterly unconventional individualist, an avowed homosexual, enemy of ties that bind, suddenly embark on this relationship? To be an agent of Joan's destiny and carry out the will of the gods to escort her to her death? To find out his own destiny once Joan had died? Whatever it was, the relationship was also wrong on an affective level. All of these more or less concealed motives existed side by side with feelings of mutual respect, admiration, and possibly love.

JOURNEY OF NO RETURN

The tone of irreverence and scorn at the apartment on 115th Street incubated like a virus, a war against multiplication tables, a crusade against comfort and complacency. It was a gathering place for a bunch of delirious souls, violent individuals, junkies, poets, killers, thieves, wastrels, time wasters, gluttons for life itself. Three of them—as written by the finger of god—were bathed in a providential aura: visionaries, emissaries from an unofficial heaven, genuine apostles of the twentieth century who will no doubt be canonized one of these millennia.

One day when everyone was high on bennies, Paul Adams, Joan's husband, showed up, having recently returned from battle in Germany. Seeing Joan and her shabby gang in tow, spewing things he failed to comprehend, sensing the disorder and upheaval of the place, he told his wife, "This is what I fought for?" Joan told him to calm down. Her furious husband ran off to file for divorce. Seeing him take off, her gaze clouded over, then she twisted her lips and smiled at her friends.

Meanwhile, the grandson of the inventor of the adding machine, the young Harvard graduate, he of the aristocratic manners and disdainful air, blasé about life, stoic suckling of *tedium vitae*, decided to rub shoulders with the riffraff of New York's lower depths and tanned his own hide with copious quantities of—oh, drugs. Armed with a revolver, syringes, ampoules, spoons, rubber bands, forged prescriptions, an overcoat and suitably shabby hat, over thirty, Burroughs had embarked on a lifelong journey of no return to the depths of himself? Hell? Oblivion? What did it matter: anywhere out of this world. But without the whiny, French-fried airs of Charles Baudelaire. Drugs, definitely, but without the clinical-redemptive motives of De Quincey, the mystical quest of Huxley or Timothy Leary. Burroughs took them straight up, just because, without justification, without any explanation beyond the very fact of doing it. So commenced the marriage between Burroughs and his substances. An unbreakable, necessary, amoral, useful, almost harmonious union, with its ups and downs, struggles, separations, where complicity is the final outcome from a narrow, mutually beneficent coexistence. Just as God needs man to assert himself, so substances needed Bill to justify their existence. Thus they helped rather than destroyed him.

New faces appeared on the scene. Ill-fated strays, rough-hewn misfits, malicious thieves, crafty grifters, all of whom fascinated William S. Burroughs and drew him like a magnet to their outsiders' realm. Burroughs delved into the malodorous catacombs of certain dark Manhattan byways, not those of Dos Passos or Salinger, nor those of Lorca or O. Henry, nor even of Henry Miller, but his very own, tinged with danger and filth, with a whiff of medicine and subways, of stalking police, of stinking puddles, of rancid taste and bitter breath. There he met Herbert Huncke, who at age fifteen had smoked marijuana and at sixteen shot heroin. A punk with a hidden soul who didn't care much for the intellectual milieu of 115th Street, gay, a repeat offender. Phil White, his mugging and shooting-up cohort with whom he would shake down the subway bums who slept on the platforms. Bill Garver, overcoat thief who sold his booty at New York pawn shops so he could buy morphine and who would later live with Burroughs in Mexico.

Joan gorged herself on Benzedrine and began to hallucinate. One day the police arrested Huncke and then Burroughs. Once again the family intervened and got him out of jail on bail. The family that lived in Saint Louis—papa Mortimer Burroughs and mama Laura Lee Burroughs, who would end up like Ginsberg's mother in an insane asylum—found out that Bill was using drugs. They didn't like it, but nothing happened: they kept sending him his two hundred dollars a month, which no longer sufficed for the three ampoules of heroin he had to take daily and which is why he resorted to shaking down bums in the subway. As no one paid Huncke's bail, he spent three months in prison. Two months later the judge sentenced Burroughs to spend a summer with his family in Saint Louis to see if this might calm him down. It was a huge punishment for Burroughs, who could not bear to spend much time in a family atmosphere.

Burroughs said good-bye to Joan and all the others, and in mid-1946 went by himself to Saint Louis. There he stopped using drugs for a time and met up with an old friend, Kells Elvins, who had fields of cotton and vegetables in Texas. The two planned to do business together. They thought they'd invent washing machines that never broke down, pills for curing cavity-ridden teeth, aphrodisiacs. The businesses never happened but Burroughs wanted easy money and got his family to give him the cash to purchase fifty acres and plant cotton in Texas. So he went to live in Pharr, a small Texas town, with Kells Elvins.

FROM PSYCHIATRIC HOSPITAL TO FARM

In New York the fellowship disbanded: Ginsberg moved, Hal Chase got fed up and left the apartment, Edie Parker moved back in with her parents, Kerouac got lost somewhere, and Joan remained alone with Julie, popping bennies in earnest. For a time Huncke joined her. Since he was gay, nothing went on between them. But Huncke introduced her to a blond, well-built, handsome man, Whitey, with whom she had a comforting affair. Huncke was now living off his various thefts, which he kept hidden in the apartment at 115th Street. One day the police knocked on the door and accused Huncke of theft and took him to the Bronx prison on 153rd Street. Joan, Whitey, and the girl were evicted for failing to pay the rent. Broke, they moved from hotel to hotel. One day Whitey tried to crack a safe and was arrested and sentenced to five to ten years at Sing Sing. Joan was left alone, sent the girl to the care of an aunt in Long Island, and went to live with a black friend of Huncke's on 47th Street, where she drowned herself in Benzedrine. Once Jack Kerouac went to see her. Failing to recognize him, Joan shouted: "Get out of my house!" She thought he was going to rape her. An astonished Jack left—Joan was out of her mind. Another day, when she was wandering around Times Square, the police picked her up and took her to Bellevue.

Ginsberg wrote Burroughs about Joan's situation and Burroughs, who said he was zealously overlooking his cotton crop in Texas, immediately flew to New York. After ten days of form filling and negotiations with the authorities, Joan left the hospital. Now that she was outside, both of them went to get Julie and decided to go to Texas. Thus began an intense period in their relationship that would continue uninterrupted until five years later. They went to live on a ranch they'd bought near New Waverly, a tiny five-block Texas town, to plant marijuana and sell it wholesale.

The ranch had no electricity, water, or neighbors. Needing a hand with field chores, Burroughs sent fifty dollars to Huncke, inviting him to work on the ranch. Huncke, who had just got out of jail, took a bus to New Waverly and went right to work. Burroughs sent him to Houston to buy marijuana seeds, as well as inhalers for Joan, and put him to work tidying the house, building wells, putting up walls and fences, hauling water. Huncke was working so much he stopped shooting up. Burroughs coordinated his workload from afar.

Joan, for her part, got high and picked raspberries. Bill killed rats and scorpions and practiced his marksmanship with a pistol. He didn't even think about writing. Burroughs was cold to Joan and they were rarely intimate; they slept in separate rooms. Julie chased armadillos and chameleons and listened to the gnome stories that her stepfather told her. In early 1947 Joan got pregnant. William Seward Burroughs III budded in her womb. Doubting that Burroughs would want the child, she asked if he wanted her to abort. Burroughs responded that abortion is murder; he was willing to have the child. Some afternoons they all sat on the porch, smoked marijuana, and listened to music from an old record player. Huncke liked Billie Holiday, Burroughs Austrian waltzes.

Meanwhile, in New York, Ginsberg and Kerouac witnessed the incarnation of the American Dionysus: Neal Cassady, who by age eighteen had been in prison ten times in Denver for auto theft. Convulsive self-taught reader, indefatigable cocksman, outrageous traveler, he swallowed women whole —men too. Back then he had a fling with Ginsberg but gave him up. Ginsberg went to the psychiatrist. Burroughs told him to try the Reichians. Kerouac was so fascinated by Neal that he made him the main character in two novels. Neal was everything Jack wanted to be but couldn't: his unattainable alter ego. Neal was amoral, Jack Catholic. Neal was unscrupulous, Jack guilt-ridden. Neal had forgotten about his mother, Jack had never been weaned. Neal was thick-skinned, Jack hypersensitive. Neal lived, Jack wrote. But they did have one thing in common: death hounded them with the same urgency. Each felt the same bony hand pushing him by the shoulder. Neal would die from an overdose of drugs and alcohol by the railroad tracks near San Miguel de Allende, Mexico, in 1968. Kerouac, a year later, hemorrhaged to death owing to excessive alcohol consumption in Florida. Both fled death at the same speed they drove. Both went after it by desperately consuming substances they were never able to use for their own benefit. Just like Burroughs.

In July 1947, in a hospital in Conroe, fifteen miles from New Waverly, William Seward Burroughs III was born without great fanfare. Because of the amount of amphetamines she was taking, Joan did not breast-feed him. A bit later, Burroughs's parents arrived at the ranch. They wanted to meet their grandson and check on their son's recovery. The stage was set. Huncke was bathed, adorned, and dressed in presentable clothing; his junkie background must not be revealed. Laura and Mortimer never got near the marijuana fields. The visit went off practically without incident. The Burroughses seemed satisfied, charmed by their grandson, assured that their son had finally begun to find his feet, to set down real perennial family roots.

A few days later, two highly distinct personalities arrived at the ranch: Allen Ginsberg and Neal Cassady. Ginsberg was in love with Neal and did everything possible to gain his favor. But Dionysus paid him no mind, humiliated him sexually and slept with Texas girls, which made Ginsberg jealous. Kicking and screaming, he could bear it no longer and left Texas. Neal stayed on the ranch.

RISKY BUSINESS IN NEW YORK

Burroughs began to consume paregoric (an opium deriva-
tive) in excess, Joan and Huncke two tubes of Benzedrine
daily. Neither Burroughs nor Huncke liked Neal. But the
marijuana harvest was in and it had to be taken to New
York. What better driver than Neal Cassady! thought Burroughs. Joan and the kids went up by train beforehand,
Huncke, Burroughs, and Neal in a jeep stuffed to the gills
with marijuana. They covered three thousand miles in three
days of nonstop driving. Neal drove most of the time. When
they got to New York, they met up with Joan at Bellevue.
She'd been accused of abandoning Julie and Billy in a train
station, where they spent a night waiting for their father.
Burroughs cleared things up and she was released. A bit
later Huncke and Burroughs descended into the lower
depths of Manhattan to unload the marijuana. But their efforts went unrewarded. As the grass hadn't been properly
dried, they were unable to sell it. The business was a flop.
They tried to improve the stuff, took it from the Bronx to
Newark, but nothing. Fed up, they sold off their harvest for
under a hundred bucks. They never grew it again. William
S. Burroughs went back to sticking a needle in his veins with
Bill Garver, the overcoat thief. On occasion they took too

much and things went wrong. Around that time, Joan's parents came for a visit. They never found out that their daughter's lover used drugs. Burroughs tried unsuccessfully to curb his addiction, then checked into a Kentucky hospital for a week and managed to kick it for a while.

In early 1948, Burroughs returned to Texas with Joan and the kids. As he no longer wanted to stay on the farm, he sold it. But before settling somewhere else, he went to Pharr, Texas, where he had cotton fields with Kells Elvins. One night, drunk, Bill and Joan took the car, parked on the side of the highway, and commenced to screw. While they were doing it, a flashlight lit up their faces. The police threw them both in jail.

Burroughs had to choose between a $173 fine and six months in the lockup. Joan asked her parents for money. Burroughs spent one night in prison. The next day the money arrived. They let him go but prohibited him from driving for six months.

LAST STOP, NEW ORLEANS

Joan and Bill left Texas and chose a place where it was easier to score drugs: New Orleans. Burroughs bought a house in

Algiers, across the Mississippi. Once there, he went back to planning businesses with Kells Elvins. They would harvest vegetables and cotton in Pharr, Texas: carrots, lettuce, peas. They hired Mexican braceros, paying them two bucks per twelve-hour day. The police shot at the Mexicans, who fled the work. In his letters, Burroughs spoke of business, described projects, tallied expenses and earnings. At night he'd go to New Orleans to score heroin, shooting up at the rate of three capsules a day. Joan displayed the first signs of polio in one leg. She used a cane and limped.

Suddenly, the American Dionysus reappeared. One day the phone rang. Burroughs answered. "I'm Helen Hinkle, the wife of a friend of Neal Cassady." Helen had nowhere to go. Burroughs took her home. Helen was alone. Two days after her wedding, her husband and Neal left Tucson, Arizona, gave her Burroughs's address and some money and headed for New York to find Kerouac and Ginsberg. Helen, a demure and somewhat prudish girl from San Francisco, got quite a jolt seeing the Burroughses in their natural state. Joan wore no bra, always walked around barefoot, inhaled Benzedrine the whole day, had insomnia, caught lizards from the trees at four in the morning, scrubbed the floors all night long, bathed and dressed up her thirteen cats though not her children, who smelled. Julie chewed on her arm so relentlessly that she had bruises on her skin. Burroughs looked like an octogenarian, locked himself in the bathroom for hours, called Billy "little beast," wore a pistol-packed holster, and tortured his cats. Joan and Bill slept in separate rooms and never touched each other. Only when they spoke were they accomplices. Joan had lost the bloom of her youth. Her face had deteriorated, she smelled of withered petals. She'd let herself go.

Weeks later, the gang reached Algiers: Neal, Kerouac, Al Hinkle, and LuAnne Sanderson, one of Neal's girlfriends. Burroughs couldn't stand Cassady: he found him noisy, self-centered, opportunistic. The man's headlong, mile-burning auto excursions annoyed him. *He* would certainly never do one. He tried to dissuade Kerouac from continuing to travel with Neal. But Jack was a devoted disciple of the American Dionysus and faithfully followed him to San Francisco. The Burroughses were left alone again.

The business in Pharr didn't pan out as planned. The peas froze and they lost five thousand dollars. The lettuce, carrot, and tomato crops sold poorly. Furthermore, Burroughs, unable to kick his heroin habit, was underwhelmed by New Orleans. There was nobody interesting around. He wrote to Ginsberg: "I have been considering the possibility of moving out of the USA to Central America, S America, or possibly to Africa" (Harris, *The Letters of William S. Burroughs*, 26).

Ginsberg replied, reproaching Burroughs for his sexual indifference toward Joan, accusing him of living a family lie. Burroughs responded that he had never hidden his homosexual preferences from Joan, that she herself controlled her own sex life. Ginsberg had a dim view of Burroughs's behavior and wanted to go to New Orleans to help him. But he never went, as certain things came up: the bacchanalian celebrations for the imminent publication of Kerouac's book *The Town and the City* and his imprisonment for being involved in Huncke and crew's various robberies, which earned him a stay at a psychiatric hospital. There he met Carl Solomon, to whom he would dedicate *Howl*, his demonic Beat poem, seven years later. Solomon had met Antonin Artaud in Paris, and so wanted to be like him that he also had electroshock therapy. The treatment was administered while he was at Pilgrim State Hospital, the same place where Allen Ginsberg's mother would end up and be lobotomized with her son's consent.

In April 1949, the New Orleans police launched a drug raid and nabbed Burroughs along with another known junkie in a stolen car. They found an unregistered pistol on him and letters to Ginsberg in which he spoke of the price of marijuana. They thought he was a drug kingpin. They entered and searched his house without a warrant and found marijuana, heroin, and a dozen weapons. They threw him back in jail. Joan got a lawyer and Burroughs got out on bail, but he was placed in a hospital to cure his substance addiction with Demerol. The cure was effective. He left the hospital within a week and felt better.

After he was released, his lawyer suggested he leave the country before his October trial date. His legal situation was problematic. A single joint of marijuana or capsule of heroin could earn you seven years in jail, so he decided to go to Pharr with Joan and the children. The business failed again because of bad harvests. The government had absurd laws for planting and selling, and the Mexican guest workers were deported, so he was no longer able to hire cheap laborers. Burroughs had had it with Fucking America. He had no other recourse than to leave the country via the shortest route possible and flee, as had Rimbaud, Lowry, John Reed, Bierce, Gauguin, and Lafcadio Hearn—but with the police shadowing him. There was no other way. Fate had called the shots. Mexico it was. Next stop: hell.

PART II

THE GODS KNOW HOW TO RUN THIS WORLD

¡VIVA MÉXICO!

Mexico City, mid-twentieth century. Maaamboooo . . . *ah uh!* Cabarets everywhere, brothels on every corner, a vibrant nightlife. Big on the scene was Pérez Prado, the pint-sized Cuban inventor of the mambo, with a face like a seal's and a Luciferesque beard, deported for playing the Mexican national anthem in mambo style. Never mind: nothing could stop the fiesta. Cha cha cha . . . *ah uh!* It was madness. Aaron Copland visits the Salón México and is enchanted by the dance hall; the muses descend and he composes one of his greatest symphonic works. Miguel Alemán allowed everything. Hell, we could go all night, the clubs never closed: Ciro's. Catacumbas. Las Veladoras. La Rata Muerta, Waikiki. Leda. Lola. Tato's. The culture of the blowout—anything goes. The Mexican Revolution had played itself out, and everyone was fed up with packing pistols and taking up arms. Civilization, señores, civilization! And partying hard. Enough already with the revolutionary ideals, banditry dressed up as a noble cause. Mexico wants peace, progress, cosmopolitanism . . . *ah uh!* More madness! Girls girls girls! Tongolele wiggles her hemispheric hips. Ninón Sevilla, the Cuban firecracker, she of the enormous mouth and huge ass, the perennial bad girl of the movies. Su Muy Key, Kalantán, Mapy Cortez, M. A. Pons . . . glamour gals, happy Afro females, sweat-glistening models, caressable lubricated specimens of the torrid tricolor night. *Aaaahhhh uh!*

Tears flowed, too, and handkerchiefs were provided. Mexicans can cry, screech, howl, and sob with the best of them. Mexicans are corny, man. Agustín Lara, with his feeble, quavery, doleful voice, the official singer of low-rent suffering. Pedro Infante, the incarnation of the brazen tough guy, inscrutable, rip-roaring idol of the maids, Mexican to the core and proud of it, with a melodramatic streak, humble but honorably coarse. Jorge Negrete, aloof denizen of the land of the eagle and the serpent, coiled up in a cactus, macho as a bottle of Cuervo tequila (for export to the USA). Thousands more, both men and women. María Félix, the dime-store diva, an overblown, haggard B-movie actress who transported the Mexican masses of the day into fits of ecstasy with her mannish vocal style and hyperartificial expressions. Thousands more. Pedro Arméndariz, elemental stud, mustachioed, pop-eyed, and ever sobbing. Marga

López, that weepy runt, the long-suffering lady wracked with guilt and beset by family burdens. And my oh my: Dolores del Río, Arturo de Córdova. All of them wept, wept, wept, like weeping willows wringing out their contrition-soaked handkerchiefs every five minutes.

Mexicans are wild and wanton, but weepy too. As much as they like to rhumba, they also love melodrama. "I'm hypermacho," they howl into the wind, then get all teary and pay homage to the goddess of self-pity.

Still, good cinema, Burroughs! You never ventured into a movie house to hear the swarthy, obese Pedro Vargas at the intermission who never moved when he sang and looked as if he was going to urinate at any moment. You never set foot inside the Cine Alameda, with lights on the ceiling like distant stars, to see the movies of Infante, Arturo de Córdova, Cantinflas, never. But take my word for it, there were some great pictures. Sure, they were sappy, but they were well made. Moralistic tearjerkers, but nicely put together. You never took Joan or Billy or Julie to the Metropolitan, the Ópera, the Lido to see the melodramas of Chachita, Pichi Fernández, or Joaquín Pardavé, the last an excellent and versatile actor if a flabby fool. Why didn't you spend a single Sunday at the Cine Orfeón, the Rivoli, the Lux, the Palacio Chino, to see *Azahares para mi boda* (Orange blossoms for my wedding) with the greatest actor of the period, Fernando Soler, or the Ritz or Hipódromo to see a film with Sara García, the heartwarming grandma of Mexican cinema? You never even took Joan to see Humphrey Bogart, Edward G. Robinson, or Lauren Bacall in *Key Largo*. Betty Grable and Dan Dailey in *When My Baby Smiles at Me*. Orson Welles and Rita Hayworth in *The Lady from Shanghai*. Bette Davis, Anne Baxter, and Marilyn Monroe in *All About Eve*. Well, you were into other things.

NATION OF COPYCATS

Mexico, mid-twentieth century. President Miguel Alemán. The first postrevolutionary president that wasn't a military man. Young, smiley, a thief, corrupt as a dung beetle, native of Veracruz, lawyer. He loved the gringos and wanted to modernize poor little Mexico. *Ah uh!* He thought of himself as a miracle worker. He attempted and succeeded to build the horrendous Miguel Alemán Viaduct in Mexico City; the grotesque Miguel Alemán apartment complex along Calle Félix Cuevas; the shocking Juárez apartment complex in the Roma district, so poorly built that it collapsed in the earthquake of 1985; the horrid La Raza hospital. He constructed hydroelectric power stations, highways, sanatoriums, monuments, etc., all horrific piles of rocks, not to mention the dreadful University City in the southern part of the Federal District, in whose center he had a statue of himself erected. Years later it was dynamited by rebellious university students in honor of his toothy grin.

During the Miguel Alemán era, urban Mexico had a model for living: the gringo model. In all its shapes and forms. Standardized American ads and appliances filled Mexico. General Motors, Kodak, Studebaker, RCA, Singer, Santa Claus, the stuffed turkey at Christmas, the little tree with ornamental balls, baseball, basketball, American football, breakfast American-style: juice, ham and eggs, coffee. In no time, the urban Mexican, freshly transplanted from the farm, adored gringo ways, which symbolized a stronger economy, modernization, fashion, privileged status. Mexicans copy. Soft drinks competed with and replaced such Mexican refreshments as *tepache*, *horchata*, orgeat, *chia*, and fresh fruit drinks. Convenience stores, how wonderful! El Ratón Macías, boxing idol of the time, endorsed Quaker Oats on TV. In the cities, Hollywood movies replaced Mexican ones. The U.S. government extended credit to Mexico.

The peso devalued against the dollar. Thousands of braceros crossed the U.S. border while thousands of American tourists crossed the Mexican border. Mexico ♥ USA and vice versa. *Time* put Diego Rivera on its cover—oh, such marvelous frescoes. Walt Disney made *The Three Caballeros:* an homage to U.S.–Latin American camaraderie. Harry Truman, president of the United States, visited Mexico. Alemán almost came in his pants and returned the favor a month later. American comics infringed on the territory of *La Familia Burrón:* Walt Disney, Nancy, Blondie, Little Lulu. In music, it was swing, Glenn Miller, Tommy Dorsey. Mexicans like to delude themselves.

Mexico was going gringo, reaffirming a penchant for refried history. For its whole life it wanted to be like its neighbor, the champion of the developed West, without managing to do so. Now, mid-twentieth century, it was America's turn, the most highly esteemed, efficient, technological, practical, advanced, and just plain awesome nation on the planetary market. Get it, kid? Fifty years from the end of the millennium Mexico wanted to be modern—but couldn't. Fifty years later, the plague persists, without the slightest effect.

ARRIVAL IN TENOCHTITLÁN

More than arriving in Mexico, William Seward Burroughs II was running from the USA. He no longer wanted to live in his homeland (his place of birth anyway). Unlike D. H. Lawrence, he wasn't interested in seeking Quetzalcóatl amid the pre-Hispanic ashes or revisiting the myths of the culture of the Aztec sun in hefty, implausible novels. Nor like Antonin Artaud did he come to rediscover the magic of ancient Mexico by trekking to the Sierra Tarahumara to ritually ingest peyote and go stark-raving mad. Nor like Graham Greene was he filing reports on Mexico or venting his hatred of the country's brutality. Nor like Aleister Crowley did he intend to scale Popocatépetl and Iztaccíhuatl via little-used trails or screw hot-blooded prostitutes or reach the thirty-sixth degree of Freemasonry. Nor like Madame Blavatsky was he on the path to wisdom. Nor like Aldous Huxley did he come to traverse the Sierra Mixteca only to get shot at by an indigenous Oaxacan stud who took offense when the author declined a shot of tequila. Nor like Vladimir Mayakovsky did he intend to meet and greet his Communist comrades. Nor like the lush Jack London did he come to send news of the gringo invasions and stay drunk all day in the cantinas of Tampico in 1914. Nor like the blessed André Breton was he planning to coauthor manifestos on the liberty of art with decrepit, washed-up political leaders. Nor like Leon Trotsky was he going to get his head split open by an ice pick. Nor like Bruno Traven would he write tales of Mexican lore. Nor like Paul Bowles would he distribute communist propaganda in Oaxaca. Nor like Hart Crane would he foreshadow his own suicide in the Gulf of Mexico hours after departing Mexican territory. Nor like Malcolm Lowry did he come to get drunk on mezcal in Cuernavaca and Oaxaca, save up his money, and write the greatest of all novels with a Mexican setting. Nor like Steinbeck did he intend to copy material so he could write little novels or mediocre Bogart screenplays. Nor was he like J. D. Salinger, who had no idea why he came to Mexico in 1952.

William S. Burroughs had other reasons for coming to Mexico. The major motivation behind Burroughs's residence in Mexico was not Mexico but Burroughs. The fact is that Burroughs could be somewhere without being there at all. He could breathe the air of a country without breathing it. Immobile traveler William S. Burroughs never budged an inch from where he stood, even if his body had been transported great distances.

In September 1949, Burroughs left New Orleans and moved to Mexico City. On September 3, the Miguel Alemán apartment complex was inaugurated at the intersection of Calle Félix Cuevas and Avenida Coyoacán; on the 8th the muralist José Clemente Orozco died. In the D.F., Burroughs surveyed the situation and rented an apartment at Paseo de la Reforma 210, no. 8, in the Cuauhtémoc neighborhood, not far from the Ángel de la Independencia monument.

His initial impression was positive: Burroughs liked Mexico. Having made arrangements, he returned to New Orleans with a good taste in his mouth. He was compelled to leave the United States quickly, as his trial was set for October 27. The Burroughses piled up their belongings, grabbed their illicit substances, gathered their follies, packed up their quirks, clung to their delusions, lunacies, oddities, costume jewelry, laid in all their interior hardware, and, with their scruffy kids in tow, arrived in Mexico City in early October. Ancient Tenochtitlán was now transformed into an undesirable cultural hybrid, an unfortunate, ill-matched, and barely compatible meeting of cultures and races. This was Mexico, a marriage between two hopelessly disparate mates: the white European race—Faustian, stupidly arrogant—and the red Mexican one—solar, savage, hallucinatory. A recipe for catastrophe.

Mexico City, Distrito Federal. 1949. A large village of two million inhabitants, with a lovely sky—blue as the eyes of the conquistadors—with pure air, white, undulating, volatile clouds, a pair of snow-capped volcanoes in the background, sparse traffic. A livable place, cheap for gringos, a little wild but welcoming. The friendliest city on earth. A bit sordid but pleasant, free of the acidity of American metropolises, a city comprised of recent arrivals from the provinces. Ridiculous if sometimes dangerous police and swindlers, tolerant if unpredictably violent authorities, an absolutely patriarchal government, a society that didn't even have the ability to spell the word *democracy*, let alone the desire to implement it, a people for whom corruption was an institution, a way of life. Their resistance was that of a woman who refuses to put on a dress that doesn't fit her.

In the beginning, Burroughs loved Mexico. He wrote to Kerouac:

> Mexico is very cheap. A single man could live good for $2 per day in Mexico City, liquor included. $1 per day anywhere else in Mexico. Fabulous whorehouses and restaurants. A large foreign colony. Cockfights, bullfights, every conceivable diversion. I strongly urge you to visit. . . . You won't make a mistake visiting Mexico. . . . One of the few places left where a man can really live like a prince. (Harris, *The Letters of William S. Burroughs*, 53, 56)

During the first few months of his stay in Mexico, Burroughs felt liberated from the constant hassles of his country. In this Aztec-Castilian land anything could be accomplished easily, he felt. The police seemed harmless and Mexicans never meddled in what did not concern them. Burroughs was not consuming drugs at the time, though he was well aware how cheap and easily obtainable they were. Joan saw fit to replace her addiction to Benzedrine with the inexpensive native tequila that she began to imbibe at eight in the morning. The kids were learning a few words of Spanish, and they were fascinated by the fanciful songs of Cri Cri, the surreal singing cricket, though they understood nothing.

Such was his initial enchantment with Mexico that William S. Burroughs wanted to buy land and once again live on his own farm where he could hunt, fish, and be self-sufficient, or open a bar at the U.S. border. And so he wanted to become a Mexican citizen. Only then, he explained, would it be possible to obtain land or start a business in Mexico. To quench his thirst for knowledge, he decided as well to find someplace where he could study Mayan and Mexica archaeology.

Far from being frightened by Mexican incivility and peculiarities, Burroughs was actually pleased by these things. He wrote to Kerouac:

Everything I have seen so far has been much to my liking. A few examples. Drunks sleep right on the sidewalk of the main drag. No cop bothers them; anyone who feels like it carries a gun. I read of several occasions where a drunken cop, shooting at the habitués in bars, were themselves shot by armed civilians who don't take no shit from nobody. All officials are corruptible; the Mexicans really like children. It is unthinkable here to be refused a room because of children; income taxes are very low; medical treatment is extremely reasonable because the doctors advertise and cut prices. You can get a clap cured for $2.40, or buy the penicillin and shoot it yourself. No regulations here curtailing self medication. Needles and syringes can be bought anywhere. These are merely a few indications of the general atmosphere of freedom from interference that prevails here.

We are living in a quiet high-class neighborhood. Everybody minds his own business such as it is. I don't know what any of the neighbors do and vice-versa. Down here curiosity is an unknown quality. People simply don't care what anyone else does. Even the landlady never asks questions. Both Willie and Julie play extensively with the neighbor's children who are well behaved in a European way. (Ibid., 62, 63)

Nor did he express the least concern in describing scenes from the Alameda Central, Mexico City's most important park, to Kerouac:

> By the way here is a quotation that might amuse you. A Sunday Supplement description of disgraceful conditions in the Alameda Park (corresponds to Central Park in NY): "Vicious people lie about on the grass drinking tequila, smoking marijuana and shouting insulting remarks at passing police officers." Quite a contrast to NY, what? (Ibid., 64)

So eager was Burroughs to find someplace unlike the United States, someplace so distinct, contrasting, and opposite, that his first vision of Mexico was quite idealized, all sweetness and light. It was what he wanted it to be, not as it would later be revealed to him. Burroughs required a credible alternative to the USA, so much so that during the early months of his residence in Mexico, he resisted seeing what might be the same as in his country, or worse. For the moment, Mexico was a miniature paradise and a chance to give the USA a good kick in the ass.

> What a relief to be rid of the US for good and all, and to be in this fine free country! I have a pistol permit (to

carry), by the way, so I don't have to take nothing off no-body. But then, nobody gives you any shit down here. I haven't been in an argument since I got here. I don't know why I didn't move down here years ago. (Ibid., 65)

But even William Seward Burroughs had his limits. Low-rent behavior left him cold. What follows is a Dantesque description of one of Mexico City's lumpen quarters, a place where he would never have resided. Burroughs verges on the scatological but isn't too bad. He confessed to Kerouac:

It is out of the question to live in a slum here. These areas compare favorably with anything in Asia for sheer filth and poverty. There are no sidewalks, people shit all over the street then lie down and sleep in it with flies crawling in and out of their mouths. Entrepreneurs (not infrequently lepers) build fires on street corners and cook up hideous, stinking nameless messes of food that they dispense to passersby. (Ibid., 63)

Allow me to quote Salvador Novo, an intellectual of exquisite refinement and acute sensibility, a smart and shrewd chronicler of Mexico at that time—even if Burroughs never heard of him. Novo provides another depiction of the atrocious conditions in downtown Mexico City of 1948:

From the corner where (the insurance firm) La Nacional is putting up a skyscraper, I walked down Santa María la Redonda to Plaza Garibaldi. The Plaza de la Corregidora has been stripped of its trees and converted into a trashy, tacky parking lot. From there, the street has been widened and is crammed with scaffolding. The large crowds assembled at the Follies spill into the surrounding streets, deafened by the blasting megaphones. There's nothing to make you want to go into the Follies; and when you walk alongside it on the way back to Calle Donceles —what an astounding, overpowering, brutish olfactory and visual display of our troglodytish gluttony! One after another: stands set up on the sidewalk hawk enchiladas and *sopes*, meat, horrendous pastries, sad-looking sweets, fly-ridden rolls; a Chinese café, yet another *taquería*, a grocery store with a window full of food, more enchiladas, more *carnitas*, fried fish, sausage, *pambazos* . . . Is there anyone who eats this crap? Who does it appeal to? There must be loads of such substandard products of the snack-and-trinket variety found on the Zócalo, all encouraged and cultivated by the authorities. (Novo, *La vida de México en el período presidencial de Miguel Alemán*, 123)

During his first months in Mexico, Burroughs was quite content. He believed in his plan, he read and recommended Wilhelm Reich, he took no drugs. His relationship with Joan and the kids was calm. He got to know the group of frivolous Americans residing in Mexico City. He didn't work; he was receiving two hundred dollars a month from his family and seventy-five more from the GI Bill (a grant that the U.S. government gave veterans to study in foreign countries). Burroughs was in fact a World War II veteran. In 1942, he enlisted in the infantry to defend his country. But instead of going to the front, he was placed in a psychiatric ward for five months to be cured of mental deterioration. It couldn't be done. Better to relieve him of his military obligations and let him go. Seven years later, Burroughs cashed in on his privileges as an ex-combatant and registered at Mexico City College to study Aztec and Maya history.

Founded in 1940 for American students, Mexico City College was at 154 San Luis Potosí, at the corner of Avenida Insurgentes in the Roma district. The courses were on Mexico: history, literature, anthropology, archaeology, economics, and so on. At that time, courses were being taught by such leading lights as José Gaos, Ignacio Bernal, Gustavo

Romero Kolbek, Antonio Alatorre, Ida Appendini, Carlos Bosch García, Justino Fernández, Jomi García Ascot, Jorge Guillén, José Luis Martínez, Pablo Martínez del Río, Edmundo O'Gorman, and Ramón Xirau. (The painter José Luis Cuevas studied at MCC during this period, paying his tuition with cartoons that were published in the college's official bulletin.) Great minds that Burroughs had never heard of. The ambience at Mexico City College was as well-mannered and complacent as a Ray Conniff record.

The gringos who studied at MCC fell into two camps. The majority were responsible and studied, did research, passed their courses with good grades, and participated in the social activities organized by the college board (innocuous costume parties, picnics, *posadas*, etc.). Then there were the rowdy ones, who traveled to Acapulco, drank to excess, chased *mexicanitas* eager for a little gringo action, and gathered daily at bars and cantinas in the Roma district and elsewhere. Burroughs obviously belonged to the latter group. He never took his studies seriously and only sporadically attended classes. Although he did take interest in his course, his main objective in registering at Mexico City College was for the economic benefits he received.

Very soon after arriving in Mexico, Burroughs had to resolve certain legal issues. One was the possibility of an extradition request, which he feared the U.S. government might serve him for not showing up at the trial that had been set for October 1949 in New Orleans. Another was his application for Mexican citizenship. He thus set out to find a lawyer. One day, while he was chatting on the phone at the Hotel Reforma in downtown Mexico City, trying to get information about it, a vaguely shady Italian fellow overheard him. After asking Burroughs what sort of legal problems he was having and discovering it had to do with drugs, he recommended a certain Bernabé Jurado. Burroughs went looking for this man, who had an office at 17 Calle Madero but often saw clients at the famous Bar Ópera on Calle Cinco de Mayo at the corner of Filomeno Mata.

What follows is a passage that Burroughs wrote for this book in 1995. The title is his own.

MY MOST UNFORGETTABLE CHARACTER

Fifty years ago, I was phoning from the lobby of the Hotel Reforma in Mexico D.F. The phone booths are open at the back and halfway of each side. I am phoning the U.S. embassy. "Could you give me the best English-speaking lawyer who handles criminal cases? Hold."

Someone taps me on the shoulder. "I couldn't help over-hearing." It was a well-dressed Italian oozing connections.

"The man you want to see is Jurado. What's your trouble? Forgery? Embezzlement?" (I guess I looked like a bank clerk.)

"No, narcotics." Yeah, enough for two shots and enough for five years on a chain gang.

"It's just a few blocks, Bill, just a bit down from Sanborns."

Sanborns is still there. I can see the American tourists from here and taste their iced tea. "I'm going to see him myself," says Tony. Right here."

I step into a universe of smiling corruption and here is the man himself. He puts his pearl handle .45 auto on a table. He is 6´3˝, broad shoulders, as a clerk in his office said, "What a man," in every sense of the word.

The man introduces me to the judge. With a diamond ring and a knowing smile.

"He protect these two *cabrones*, wanted in Peru." The well-dressed plump cabrones nod and *smile*. And this man Jones, wanted in Chicago, flips a hat from the toe of his shoe. It lights on his head. He lifts the hat and smiles.

A year of smiles later, Bernabé Jurado told me: "I saw the judge and gave him some money, too.

"I will marry you with a Mexican woman. The gentlemen from Peru bear witness."

"We aim to please," they say.

Later had trouble in Mexico. Bernabé gets me out on permanent bail. I have to sign every week.

Later, Bernabé shoots some kid grazed his Cadillac. He lays out some money. All clear, except the kid dies two weeks later from tetanus. So Bernabé takes a long holiday and the office wants more.

"But I gave."

"The situation has changed many times since then," one of the lawyers at the office tells me, stroking his mustache.

Only later did I realize what I had learned from Bernabé Jurado. Every man can make his own universe of smiles if (he) can smile strong enough and smile long enough. You see, he's *already there.*

"You know me, *friend.*"

Maybe he could. Can death be a friend? Can a man have a friend? Be a friend? Every man *can* make his own universe. Every man is then limited by the laws of the universe he has made. Fourteen wives? That's stretching things a bit.

Time hits the hardest blows.

"I eat too much, I drink too much, and I fuck too much," Jurado used to say.

It was in his office I met Old Ike and got back on junk. Tony had a beautiful, red-headed girlfriend. Some deal on in Acapulco.

THE DEVIL'S ADVOCATE

Bernabé Jurado. The devil's advocate, the ultimate scam artist, cynical king of the bribe, Mexican lawyer in extremis, defender of thugs and the defenseless. He was born in Durango in 1910. His father was owner of the hacienda of Canutillo. In 1915, Pancho Villa appropriated the hacienda, took his father prisoner, and shot him in front of his family. Before the man was riddled with bullets, the young Bernabé ran to Villa, knelt before him, and wrapped his arms around the rebel's legs, imploring: "Don't kill my father!" The merciless Villa grabbed the boy and kicked him out of the way.

Later on, Bernabé accompanied his mother and sister to Minas Nuevas, Chihuahua, where he labored in a mine fourteen hours a day to support his family. At age twelve he went to Mexico City. As a teenager, he played American football. During one game, he was kicked in his private parts so severely that he was left sterile, and he never had any children. He also played soccer, becoming a top player for Club Asturias.

Bernabé studied accounting, medicine, and law. He graduated in 1937 after writing a thesis on labor law. He began to practice law as a clerk, defending striking workers. He learned his moves from con men, then became a master of the trade himself. That's just how things are in Mexico.

Jurado was also an unrepentant womanizer and he married fourteen times. Like Neal Cassady, he consumed women whole, in a single bite. At a party at the Corinto (later the Waikiki), on Paseo de la Reforma near the Caballito horse sculpture, Bernabé approached a prominent couple as they moved drunkenly across the dance floor. The woman, Alma Valente, was the frisky sister of former Mexican president Abelardo Rodríguez's wife. Coming up to the woman's suitor, who had his arms wrapped tremulously around the feverish Alma's waist, Bernabé said, "Do you realize you're dancing with the loveliest piece of ass in Mexico?"

Bernabé's love was Adelina Hill, daughter of the revolutionary general Benjamín Hill, and he married her twice.

Jurado liked cocaine, liquor, cantinas. He divorced Lupe Marín from Diego Rivera, Pedro Infante from María Luisa

León, and Manuel Medel from Rosita Fornés; Medel despised him for it. When a journalist libeled him, he sought out the man, showed him the offending article, and urinated on it. Bernabé Jurado's way was multifaceted but always crooked. His mottos: "Win, come hell or high water, buy off judges, bribe witnesses, doctor documents, threaten prosecutors, challenge them to duels, beat on your opponents when litigating."

During one trial, he asked the judge for evidence against his client: a bounced check. Jurado took the check and swallowed it. His client was released for lack of evidence.

Bernabé Jurado went to jail only once, a year before he departed this world.

In June 1980, in a fit of jealousy, he killed his wife in his penthouse at No. 3 Calle Varsovia in the Zona Rosa. Later he put a large bullet into his own temple. He died instantly. It was his final scam.

When Burroughs entered the office of Jurado—who was not, as some biographers assert, the brother of the actress Katy Jurado—he saw a giant of a man of around forty, black hair, well-built, impeccably dressed, macho, and mustachioed with a sage gaze. Burroughs explained his case. Jurado said he would help him. Little could the lawyer imagine that a year and a half later he would have to summon all of his skills to spring this odd gringo from prison, this lean, inscrutable figure of aristocratic manners standing before his desk, who, like him, would kill his wife with a pistol. Nor that years hence, this same gringo would become one of the most important literary visionaries of the twentieth century.

A WRITER'S BEGINNINGS

At the start of 1950, Burroughs turned thirty-six: on the fifth of February, anniversary of the implementation of the Mexican Constitution of 1917, of which Mexicans remain curiously proud. Burroughs wrote Ginsberg long and didactic letters reproaching him for wanting to "overcome" his homosexuality, for setting up a false dichotomy between normal life and visionary life. He lectured Ginsberg on ethics, sexology, and politics, bashed liberalism and communism, defended cooperativism, insisted that Allen be true to himself, criticized him for reflexively following the line of others. He believed in telepathy and life after death. The tone of his lessons was harsh; each time he told off an obtuse and timid Ginsberg, who was too fearful to accept himself.

Burroughs was less paternalistic and preachy with Ker-

ouac, maintaining a more aloof tone. Kerouac had just published his first novel, *The Town and the City*, which Burroughs liked. Burroughs read Wilhelm Reich often, constructed three orgone boxes, and, prompted by his friend
Kells Elvins, began to write his first novel, *Junky*, on his experience with drugs. He wrote daily at home and had a secretary type it up from his dictations. Instead of typing the
word *junk*, the secretary insisted on typing *opiates*. Burroughs angrily corrected her: he wanted *junk*, not *opiates*.

Burroughs decided to write under the influence of certain
substances. His decision to make literature was a dispassion-
ate one; it wasn't driven by an irrepressible urge to put pen
to paper and give up everything. It was not even a confirma-
tion of a creative, fatal vocation born of a dependency as
powerful as that of any drug. It was simply a form of mum-
bling, an early indication of what would later become a
curse. Burroughs wrote, but didn't place much importance
on the act. He wasn't vitally committed to the text, it didn't
spring from his guts or mental precipices. William S. Burroughs wrote and could live perfectly well without doing so.
He had broached a heavy subject—consuming and trafficking in drugs—from afar, without getting his soul involved. It
was nicely done, in a simple, linear style. This was not a fully
dressed Burroughs, with all his thunder, vision, and spells.

Junky is a cold text. It isn't autobiographical and it is autobiographical. Reconstructed from Burroughs's misadventures in the world of drug addiction, the account doesn't adhere too closely to actual events. Real characters come and go, their names changed. Kerouac and Ginsberg never appear. Burroughs doesn't tell everything that happened, nor did everything happen that he tells. His individuality clearly emerges throughout the text, as does the odd distance that separates him from Joan, who shows up only a few times in the book. *Junky* is a pre-Burroughsian work. The inventor of the impossible-to-decipher cosmos, minstrel of howling and shrieking your head off, compulsive excreter of indigo and purple farts, shaman of the age of vitriol, saurian sorcerer who exalted other gods, death's accomplice, scheming emissary from beyond, would only arise years later, in Africa, with *Naked Lunch*. Meanwhile, in Mexico City, William S. Burroughs, without realizing it at all, was honing his skills to dare to transcend the material world.

All Burroughs did in Mexico was write. He had no desire to produce culture or form literary circles, much less academic or intellectual ones. Burroughs never had any interest in modern Mexican culture, never exchanged a word with the leading lights of the era, never attended a conference or play. He may never have even purchased a book written by a Mexican. Forty years afterward, he had never heard mention of Octavio Paz, Carlos Fuentes, or Juan Rulfo. If by some chance he ever looked at the frescoes of our illustrious muralists on the walls of the National Palace of Fine Arts or the Hotel del Prado, he didn't care for them. Burroughs remained aloof from Mexico's cultural fireworks. He had other interests. More than artists or intellectuals, it was the bizarre characters of Mexico's underworld that fascinated him: Jurado, Lola la Chata, David Tesorero.

He hadn't a clue that during those years Octavio Paz's *Libertad bajo palabra* (Freedom on parole), *The Labyrinth of Solitude*, or *Eagle or Sun* was published, that José Revueltas's *Los días terrenales* (Earthly days) came out, that José Ortiz de Montellano, Xavier Villaurrutia, and José Clemente Orozco died, that the centennial of the death of Manuel Acuña was pompously and solemnly observed, that Juan José Arreola's *Varia invención* (Various inventions) and Artemio de Valle Arizpe's *La Güera Rodríguez* (The Fair Rodríguez) were published, that the National Conservatory was built by Mario Pani, that Fernando Benítez directed the "México en la Cultura" supplement to *Novedades* newspaper, or that Mariano Azuela received the National Literary Prize in 1949. Nor did he hear that José Rubén Romero flew into a rage when Carlos Chávez, at that time director of the National Institute of Fine Arts, awarded the distinction to Azuela, that Wolf Ruvinskis and María Douglas performed in the Mexican production of Tennessee Williams's *A Streetcar Named Desire*; that Miguel Córcega appeared in Sartre's *Dirty Hands*; that *Rosalba y los llaveros* by Emilio Carballido, just a lad at the time, was staged; or that Manuel Esparza Oteo passed away (on Burroughs's birthday) in 1950. Nor was he aware that Sergio Magaña premiered his play *Los Signos del Zodíaco*; that Leonard Bernstein conducted the National Symphony Orchestra's interpretation of *Jeremiah*, *El Salón México*, and *Sinfonía India* by Carlos Chávez at the Palace of Fine Arts; that a banquet in Bernstein's honor was held at the Hotel del Prado; that Salvador Novo's play *La Culta Dama* was staged; that David Siqueiros painted *Cuauhtémoc Revivido*; that Virginia Fábregas died, or that in April 1951 a Congress of the Academies of the Spanish Language was held in Mexico City.

In this sense, Burroughs had already become Burroughs. A man apart from the fireworks and fanfare of culture, aloof from the official academic or intellectual currents of planet Earth. William S. Burroughs had ever been like this and would continue to be so, in Tangier, Paris, London, New York, Lawrence. In Mexico, Burroughs slithered silently and inexorably, like a shadow, at the edge of the crowd. *El hombre invisible.* Neither high nor low culture appealed to him. Not Alfonso Reyes, not Pérez Prado, not Diego Rivera, not Tongolele. Pre-Hispanic culture perhaps, or the lower depths and druggy atmosphere of Mexico City, but nothing else. Burroughs had no Mexican friends, except for the youth that became his occasional lover, Angelo, whom he used to bring to his bachelor apartment at Río Lerma 26, a place that he used for that purpose for a time. He never went dancing at Ciro's, the Catacumbas, the Rata, a club located on the Callejón Federico García Lorca opposite the Benito Juárez monument. His pals were rowdy gringos who, like him, supposedly studied at Mexico City College. Drifters, screwy Yankees who staged monumentally boozy bashes. Zero Mexican pals. Lowry had his Mexican friends. Breton and Mayakovsky certainly rubbed shoulders with the sacred cows of their day. Even Lawrence made attempts to interview prominent public figures. Not Burroughs. William S. Burroughs was in Mexico but he remained far, far away from it.

THE USUAL SUSPECTS

And while he was writing *Junky*, he returned to drugs. One day he was in the reception area of Jurado's office when he saw a short, slovenly man of around fifty. He knew straight-away that he was a junkie—addicts could easily sniff out one another. Dave Tesorero, Old Dave, was his name, Ike in *Junky*, a twenty-five-year addict, Chicano, seller of suppos-edly silver jewelry. Skilled in the art of scoring drugs, he had a Mexican girlfriend who was also an addict: Esperanza Villanueva, about whom Kerouac would produce a novel in 1956, *Tristessa*. That day they dined together on San Juan de Letrán. While they were having dessert, Tesorero invited Burroughs to shoot up. Burroughs accepted.

A little while later, Burroughs brandished the syringe and sank it into his veins. Within a few days he had a thrice-daily habit and urgently needed to score. Tesorero gave him the lowdown: in Mexico City there was a monopoly. One woman controlled the black market: Lola la Chata, Lupita in *Junky*. She alone sold drugs in the Federal District. No one else. Whoever dared to compete with her was, on her orders, summarily apprehended by the police whom she'd bought out. Bribery, control. But Lola's stuff was costly and of poor quality—it was diluted. Instead of heroin, she sold pantopon cut with sugar or powdered milk, which stuck to the spoon when it was heated. A packet of heroin cost fifteen pesos. Burroughs found that expensive because he had to purchase two to four per day.

Burroughs and Tesorero sought other ways to obtain drugs. Prescriptions, for example. They contacted doctors to write prescriptions for codeine (an opiate) for patient Bill and patient Dave. The doctors didn't hesitate to sign; they had to eat. Burroughs and Tesorero started going to downtown pharmacies to get these scripts filled. Few employees fell into that trap. "We don't serve addicts," they snapped, and Bill and Dave split. So they looked for pharmacies in Mexico City's poorer quarters, which weren't quite so finicky. They showed the prescription, got the codeine, and deposited it in their bloodstream. Tesorero was a master at injecting—not a vein resisted—unlike Burroughs, who at times had to remove his shoe and sink the needle into one of the veins in his feet, unable to find others he could penetrate.

Then, suddenly, a blessing! Bill and Dave discovered a heaven-sent method for obtaining morphine. Curiously, the Ministry of Health started issuing morphine prescriptions to addicts who needed the substance. All that was required was a private doctor's prescription and some cash, and each month the applicant would receive fifteen grams, at two dollars a gram. Bill and Dave made a request, gave a doctor a hundred pesos, and within ten days they were issued a box full of morphine ampoules. Terrific, thought Burroughs, who had never seen so much morphine in one place in the

United States. The same quantity that would've gone for three hundred dollars back home cost thirty in Mexico City.

Burroughs wallowed in drugs, becoming more self-absorbed than ever. His sexual appetite, never too strong with Joan, languished further. His scant sociability waned entirely. Burroughs retreated into himself. He caught and tortured cats, his energy turned centripetal. While he realized he was enslaved by these substances, he was powerless to kick. Joan got hysterical. One time Dave was picked up for vagrancy and thrown in jail for fifteen days. When Burroughs visited him, Old Dave looked gaunt, puny, emaciated. He hadn't shot up in seventy-two hours. Burroughs went to the jail with a piece of opium wrapped in cellophane hidden under his tongue. He also had an orange in his hand with opium concealed between the wedges. When he handed over the drugs, Dave jumped for joy, then ran back to his cell and somehow put the enchanted substance into his body.

When Dave got out of prison, he and Burroughs went to Chalma, a small town one hundred kilometers outside Mexico City, on foot, all the way stoned on morphine. It took them two days to get there. There was a chapel devoted to the Lord of Chalma and next to it one for the lady of grifters, petty thieves, addicts, and other shady characters, who arrived at the altar on their knees and left offerings, including small bags of dope. Tesorero had brought along twenty packets of morphine to sell. He stood beside the altar, sniffed out the junkies, gave them a wink, and offered the drugs. Their first night in Chalma, Bill and Tesorero slept in a hayloft on a farm. In the morning, their hostess invited them for blue tortillas, eggs *à la mexicana*, and coffee. Bill was delighted by the breakfast, if not the freak show of pilgrims who dragged up, crawled, begged, and prayed so needfully to the Lady of Chalma.

LOLA LA CHATA

A brief look at the life of a heroine of the Mexican underground.

Lola la Chata. María Dolores Estevez Zulueta. That tremendous, obese, big mama, 4½ feet tall, 120 kilos. Coatlicue (she of the serpent skirt) of Mexican drug culture, empress of the contraband trade through the 20s, 30s, 40s, and 50s, the grande dame of the narcos, queen bee of the black market, owner of the largest underground drug monopoly in Latin America. She was variously accused of trading in illegal substances, poisoning innocent bodies, perverting the human race, and promoting perdition. She died on September 4, 1959, and was born on the Friday of Sorrows, 1906, in Mexico City.

Little Lola lived in a modest apartment complex on Calle Rosario in the district of La Merced. To survive, she helped her wretched mother sell stewed *chicharrón* and spiked coffee from a street stall on Carretones Street, at the corner of Talavera and Alhóndiga, there in La Merced. At age thirteen, her mother used Lola as a *burro*, that is, a drug dealer of marijuana, morphine, and heroin, which she hawked from the stall. In the evenings, Lola got to know the thug Casto Ruz Urquizo, with whom she eloped to Ciudad Juárez. There she gave birth to two daughters, Dolores and María Luisa, and fell in with the border narcos, picking up the tricks, scams, and moves of the subterranean drug world. Lola la Chata never learned to read or write; she only knew how to keep the books.

Having undergone her trial by fire, she went back to Mexico City and set up general headquarters for the distribution of narcotics on Calle San Simón, in La Merced. She became an artist of the bribe. She had bought officials from the Narcotics Bureau and high-ranking members of the police force. Lola was a magnanimous queenpin, however. During the Lenten period, she filled a truck with fish and had it delivered to the inhabitants of La Merced. People loved her, respected her, protected her.

Beginning in 1934, Lola landed in jail six times: at the Lecumberri Palace, at Islas Marías, and in the Women's Prison. On July 6, 1945, she was arrested and sent to Islas Marías. There she constructed a hotel and an airport so her daughters could fly in for a visit. Lola was released from Islas Marías with a medical certificate stating that she was ill. Transferred to Lecumberri, she managed to get out thanks to her skill in pulling strings and working the legal loopholes. She sent her daughters to Canada to do their studies.

Lola was a highly religious Catholic and devotee of the Virgin of San Juan de los Lagos. Each year she would go to this pilgrimage site in a car full of flowers with three or four truckloads of La Merced inhabitants, all expenses paid.

Lola's business was perfectly organized. Distribution was handled through vendors who hid the drugs in printed prayer notes or under the sides of plastic yo-yos. The narco empress had distribution and sales centers in several key places around Mexico City, such as Callejón de San Ciprián, the Tepito district, La Mosqueta, and Cerrada San Nicolás, as well as 255 Camelia, in the Guerrero district, where her second husband Enrique Jaramillo had a machine shop.

She distributed drugs throughout Mexico's other states in the same fashion.

To protect herself from police activity, besides offering lavish bribes to countless cops, she hindered their operations. For example, she had spies placed at numerous police stations to look in on high officials. These moles kept her abreast of the shady dealings that were plotted on in these places.

Although all kinds of men liked Lola, she married the ex-cop Enrique Jaramillo, alias El Güero, a good-looking guy who she loved but had to divorce out of security concerns: she wanted to protect him from police harassment and other risks. The only thing between Lola and Enrique was prison; otherwise they were always together.

On the afternoon of April 4, 1957, twenty-five agents from the Federal Judicial Police, armed to the teeth with machine guns, submachine guns, gas bombs, and automatic pistols, all under the command of the force chief, Lieutenant Colonel Armando Valderrain, surrounded the house at 155 Teseo in the Prado Churubusco district. The property belonged to Lola la Chata, who at that moment, together with her six servants, was cooking up a big meal. From outside, the troops shouted that Lola should turn herself in. Lola wanted to escape but was unable to; the house was totally surrounded. She finally let the police come in and get her. When the head of the operation approached her, she offered him two hundred thousand pesos to let her go. The policeman refused. They were rough on her. There was nothing left for the leading drug trafficker in Latin America to do but turn herself in peacefully and go along with the agents. She asked only one thing: that they let her drive her car, a late-model Nash, to transport herself to the station. The agents agreed.

Because they found heroin in her house, Lola pretended during the trial to be a drug addict, a heroin fiend, not a trafficker, and, as she was being questioned, she acted out tremendous dramas worthy of the hardest of addicts to make them think she really needed to shoot up all the time. She had no patience or respect for judges. Once when a judge pressed her to speak, Lola picked up a typewriter that was on the desk and hurled it at the official, who fell back spectacularly. General hilarity resounded in the courtroom.

Lola wore dark glasses to the trials, her head draped in a shawl. She hated journalists who persisted in calling her a criminal. No sooner would she see them than she'd tell them to go fuck themselves. At another interrogation, a judge who felt he'd been offended slapped her. A year later, when Lola was in jail, the same judge went to her to request a loan for one thousand pesos because his wife had died and he had no money for the burial. Lola told him: "Listen, you son of a bitch, despite everything and that you slapped me, I'm going to give you the damn thousand pesos, but it's for your wife, not you," and she tossed the bills on the floor. Lola was fair and just. Among other charges, Lola was accused of having ties to other drug kingpins in Mexico such as Pancho Pistolas, Pedro Sosa Belmont, and Max Cossman, all in jail. She denied the charges: "I don't need to make allies with anyone," she stated.

Lola was sentenced to four years in prison. The authorities would supposedly follow up her incarceration by tracking down officials who colluded with her. Just one was mentioned: the head of the Federal Narcotics Police, Humberto Mariel Lazo, who was never arrested. Lola was sent to the Women's Prison in Iztapalapa to do her time.

In prison, Lola got up every day at 5 a.m. Her two maids bathed her and made her up with extreme care. She appreciated fine cuisine and, out of her own pocket, had meals prepared for the inmates. She also rented films that were regularly shown in the penitentiary's theater. Every month, a stylist dyed her hair black, and on Christmas she bought piñatas, installed an enormous Christmas scene, and paid for a sumptuous dinner for all the prisoners, who adored her for it, as well as for covering burials and all sorts of other expenses.

Each Wednesday, thirty to forty people would visit and ask her for assistance. The altruistic Lola dealt out cash, advice, and protection to whoever asked her for it. She herself never used drugs, either inside or outside jail. Lola went about the prison decked out in jewels, watches (she had sixty-five, of every description), silk shawls (she owned an international collection), gold bracelets. She liked to flash a smile and show off her dazzling inlays and she used to stash a million-peso wad in her bra.

Lola passed away on September 4, 1959, not from an overdose of heroin, which she never used (they said she was more addicted to trading drugs than addicts were to consuming them), but from a heart attack as a result of a bladder operation, which she agreed to have because she didn't want to smell. All of the inmates wept. The wake was held in Gayosso and she was buried at Dolores Cemetery. Attending the service were innumerable agents, police, judges, and officials who'd benefited from her favors and wanted to pay their last respects. Of the five hundred people in attendance, two hundred were policemen hoping to spot any likely suspects at the scene.

William S. Burroughs never met Lola. He saw her as an

invariably shadowy presence in the drug market of Mexico City, and although he didn't buy much dope from her, Lola la Chata always held a fascination for him: her underground character, her masterful ability to elude the law, her lack of respect for the police, like a Mexican Dillinger. Lola shows up in at least three of Burroughs's novels: *Junky*, *Naked Lunch*, and *Cities of the Red Night*. In 1992, this author gave Burroughs a photo of Lola that the writer had never seen before. So impressed was he by the photo that he produced a montage in which it appears as a central motif and exhibited it around the world. He entitled it *Folk Heroes*. No doubt, Lola, from the heavens, would smile contentedly upon learning of Burroughs's interest in her, flashing her jewel inlays.

EXCITABLE JOAN

In mid-1950, Burroughs and family moved to No. 37 Cerrada de Medellín (now Calle José Alvarado), behind the Sears Roebuck in the Roma district. Burroughs, hooked on drugs, only rarely went to Mexico City College, whose students struck him as a pack of bores. Joan continued to down tequila, limped and had to use a cane, much weakened and at the same time fed up with her husband's addiction. At times, she became intolerant, and once, while Bill was setting up a shot of morphine, Joan grabbed the spoon in which the substance floated, ready to be dispensed into the syringe, and angrily hurled it to the floor. An irate Bill withheld his usual respect for Joan and slapped her face twice. In tears, she of the faded charms told the infuriated Bill that he'd lost control: "Don't you want to do anything at all? You know how bored you get when you have a habit. It's like all the lights went out. Oh well, do what you want. I guess you have some stashed, anyway."

Actually, Bill did have more drugs, but this time Joan went further and spoke of a separation. For the first time since they'd been together the couple seemed to be cracking at the seams because of Joan, who at age twenty-six seemed more deteriorated than ever. Why did she stay with William S. Burroughs, who never treated her as a wife, a lover, a woman? Sexual intimacy between them was nonexistent. But she'd been warned: Bill had never promised her a blissful marriage, nor even a familial connection or a "normal" sex life. What did Joan see in William S. Burroughs? Why didn't she dump him, return to the United States, raise the kids, and start a new life alone? Have a career, supporters, etc. Why the hell didn't she get away? Why had her life from the time she joined Bill degenerated precipitously into a dynamic cycle of self-destruction and decay? Joan deserved Burroughs; she chose him, after all. What did she choose? Death. Burroughs meant death to Joan, her own death. Not stability or protection or raising a family or a compatible marriage, no quest for a shared adventure.

Joan wanted to die and Bill served as her escort to the final precipice. Further still, he would be the executor of her fate. What better companion toward the darkness than William S. Burroughs, over whom death loomed every minute of his life, like a swarm of mosquitoes around his head, like a black aura enveloping his body? Death was always breathing down his neck, though he never succumbed in desperation. Bill was a leathery reptile with an incredible ability to plunge to the depths and surface unscathed. Not Joan. Joan was tender. Her intelligence and clarity were not made of the same bullet-proof stuff as Burroughs's. Joan was more like Kerouac: life seemed too large for them. Neither could face the world, neither could deal squarely with it, so it destroyed them—in different ways, but in the same measure.

She didn't follow in the footsteps of Jan Lowry, Malcolm's wife, who fifteen years earlier had gone through something similar in Mexico. Jan left her besotted husband when she could no longer stand living with him. She left him alone to drown his sorrows in the cantinas of Cuernavaca.

She simply split, placing herself before her adrift husband, and remade her life. Joan didn't leave Bill because, unlike Jan, she did not want to live. There's no way of knowing how conscious was this attitude of hers, how perversely determined her decision. She simply wanted to die, like others who cannot bear life, who see no sense in suffering, who never touch down, and who say, "To hell with it all!" In this passage to self-negation, Joan kept Bill at her side to help forge her demise.

Nevertheless, this time Joan was feeling fed up and wanted to break with Burroughs. But it was just a fleeting outburst. Joan lacked the determination to achieve a definitive separation. Besides, her fleeting impulse to break with Burroughs was interrupted by the appearance of some American friends who suddenly arrived in Mexico.

ON THE ROAD

In the summer of 1950, Jack Kerouac and Neal Cassady crossed the border from Laredo, Texas, to Laredo, Tamaulipas. Their intense, speedy, slam-bang, epic journeys had until then been limited to gringo territory. Mexico was a revelation to them.

"We had finally found the magic land at the end of the

road and we never dreamed the extent of the magic," wrote Kerouac at the end of *On the Road*, astonished at how cheap life was across the border and how easy it was to get girls, witnessing the naturalness and calmness of the Mexicans, the essential, almost messianic nature of the Indians, the benevolence and harmlessness of the police, seeing how easy it was to score marijuana, hearing the "world beat" in the mambos of Pérez Prado. The Mexico they found was an almost biblical land.

After clearing the border, Jack and Neal headed for the whorehouses of Gregoria, Tamaulipas, got drunk, smoked enormous joints, and finally arrived in Mexico City, where, as Kerouac told it, they found a sort of underdeveloped wonderland where the indigenous panorama—street tacos, pulque, Indians driving cars—amazed and pleased the pair of exhausted gringos. They were fascinated by a land that, at least superficially, was entirely different from and far better than the USA.

Neal had gone to Mexico to divorce his second wife, Kerouac to visit Burroughs and Joan. Jack's enchantment was short-lived. Arriving at Burroughs's place, he began to feel ill. He'd picked up a case of dysentery, had a lingering fever, and was bedridden for days. Having obtained his divorce, Neal left the ailing Kerouac, got in his old Ford from the thirties, and returned to the United States to get married for the third time, in New York. Jack stayed two months in Burroughs's house, compulsively drinking and smoking marijuana the whole time. Never had he put away so much booze and dope. He shut himself in his room and drank and smoked, alone, every day, without writing a word. Nothing but getting stoned and drunk. The Mexican paradise so idyllically and enthusiastically described in *On the Road* seemed more a literary device than something he'd actually lived through.

Shortly after Kerouac left the hallowed ground of Mexico and returned to New York, Burroughs—now deeply into drugs—wrote to him, and with the utmost tact told him to calm down, to go easy, and that as a young man free of vices, he shouldn't throw his life away on such excesses. Words from a seasoned pro on the subject.

THE SCORPION

Burroughs continued to shoot up while attempting to kick the habit. He tried to obtain Mexican citizenship (though Jurado couldn't swing it) so he could plant crops and be self-sufficient, something he was unable to do in the USA. Meanwhile, his eyes were opening to the Kafkaesque nature of the Mexican institutions charged with processing documents . . . "I am still in process of getting my citizenship papers. The immigration dept is like Kafka. Fortunately I have retained a competent advocate skilled in the interstices of bureaucratic procedures" (ibid., 69). He continued to detest the United States, and worked on *Junky* while residing at Cerrada de Medellín 37. In the midst of all this, Lucien Carr, that Rimbaudian lad who'd left jail four years before and now worked in publishing, showed up with his girlfriend at Burroughs's place. It was a brief visit but time enough for him to notice an interesting aspect of the Joan–Bill relationship. Lucien was witness to a strange game performed by the Burroughses at their apartment in the Roma district. Joan sat in one corner of the room, Bill in another. Each took out a sheet of paper and pencil and drew a box divided into nine equal squares. In each square, they drew an image, and when they'd finished they compared their work. The results were startling. More than half the images matched. Between Joan and Bill, he thought, there was a special, profound degree of communication guided by the power that Joan exerted over Bill. She was the transmitter, he the receiver.

Then, another friend of Bill's turned up: Kells Elvins, his

old farming partner from Texas, accompanied by wife Marianne, who was pregnant at the time. The Elvinses rented an apartment alongside the Guadalajara exit off Ávila Camacho Boulevard. Business in Texas hadn't paid off as he'd thought it would. So he sold his land and went to Mexico with the intention of taking a few courses. Years earlier he had studied with Erich Fromm in Cuernavaca. Kells was prone to alcoholism, headstrong, extroverted, womanizing, irascible, and well-dressed. He was a lover of beautiful, if rather traditional, women and a writer in training, openminded with a dash of anticonservatism, though deep down he was quite conventional. The differences between him and Burroughs were obvious. Still, the two shared a bond of friendship that, despite the distances, lasted many years until Kells's death in 1961. But they saw little of each other in Mexico, because of Marianne's discomfort with the Burroughses.

Marianne Elvins's comments on the Burroughses in Mexico seem quite similar to those of Helen Hinkle in 1948 when she was in New Orleans. Like Helen, Marianne had recently married and remained somewhat prudish and conventional. On one occasion, the Elvinses invited the Burroughses to dinner at the apartment and Marianne was shocked. Here's her account of the evening:

In 1950, Kells and I rented a modern apartment in Mexico City. It was there where the Burroughses visited us for the first time. I don't remember anything about our conversations, maybe because William and Joan were so drunk that every word they used was quite incoherent or maybe because their appearance made myself not to want be involved with them.

Joan was a big woman, shapeless, with puffed face and impressive blue eyes, with the lost expression of the old doll's glass eyes. Her expression reflected everything but saw nothing. She seemed very receptive and shy, like a kind of mental patient who was free in the afternoon.

Burroughs had a cadaverous appearance: thin lips, bad teeth, eyes like death. Once, Kells and I went to Acapulco with another couple to a very well known place, and when the bellboy opened the door of the bungalow there was a scorpion on the tile floor. I had never seen a scorpion in my life, but soon I realized it was something evil. The same thing I felt about Bill Burroughs.

For some reason, that afternoon in our apartment, Bill and Joan sat on a sofa in front of us. Suddenly, Joan's bag fell onto the floor and a lot of pills of many colors and shapes spread on the carpet. Clumsily, Joan crawled on the carpet, picked up her things with both hands and smiling and muttering to herself returned all the stuff to her bag. Kells and Bill never paid attention to all of this.

Another episode I remembered took place in Burroughs' home. We went to have dinner with them and Joan cooked a roast beef almost raw, put it in front of Bill and when he saw it he attacked the meat as if it was a wild animal, pulling up the pieces and throwing them to our dishes. The last thing I remembered of that day was Bill taking a piece of meat and devouring it completely.

At that time in Mexico I was very young, I was not very open-minded and I was pregnant for the first time. The idea to share my time with that crazy couple was something that I couldn't stand. I think Kells must have understood that because he never forced me to see them. (Interview with Ted Morgan, unpublished)

NOT SO LOVELY AND BELOVED MEXICO

While television was making its debut in Mexico in late 1950 and the Pan-American Highway opened, while the flow of gringo tourism to Mexico increased enormously and thousands of Mexican braceros were crossing their northern border in search of work—"They keep going in as masters and departing as slaves," wrote Salvador Novo—Burroughs continued consuming drugs, writing *Junky*, frequenting the bars of the Roma district, and experiencing disappointment toward his onetime Mexican paradise. In fact, Burroughs was starting to hate lovely and beloved Mexico. He was noticing that behind the goodwill, the respectfulness, good cheer, warmth, and tolerance crouched a monstrous dose of irresponsibility, chiefly in terms of bureaucracy. This was partly owing to the fact that he'd given a thousand dollars to the Mexican Department of Immigration in late 1950 so he could legally settle down in Mexico but got nothing in return.

Suddenly, Bill's plans for Mexico were beginning to unravel. His desire to buy a farm in Mexico, plant crops, hunt, fish, be self-sufficient, and live on next to nothing—something quite different from the individualist and collectivist utopia of Lawrence—came toppling down because of the legal impossibility of doing so. And so he had to set his sights on someplace else where his Thoreau-inspired dreams might actually be realized. In January 1951, Burroughs wrote to Ginsberg:

> I have about decided to move on South—probably to Panama or possibly Ecuador. There are plenty of countries down here that want Americans to come to farm, so

I do not see any point in waiting more time in a country that does not want American immigrants. . . . I am returning briefly to the US for a tourist card. I will return here, take the cure, and go on from here to wherever I decide to go. (Unpublished letter)

Evidently, Burroughs did not go to the United States right away for a tourist card or to take the cure, nor did he even leave Mexico. But his disappointment was abundantly clear. The idyllic Mexico that he thought he'd find was showing its true colors: it was a slacking, irresponsible, ambivalent, restrictive place that bucked like a bull. It was a tough nut to crack. From this point on, Burroughs's feelings about Mexico were uneven: now he liked it, now he hated it.

Such ambivalence has been quite common among European and American writers who set foot on Mexican soil in the twentieth century, as attracted as they were repelled by the land of the eagle and the serpent. Generally, they liked Mexico's "innocence," its naturalness, its hybrid nature and preservation of traditions. These were things that didn't exist in first-world countries. Paradoxically, the practical effects of these same features often upset them.

THE TORTURED CAT

By December 1950, Burroughs had completed a draft of *Junky*. He immediately sent it over to Lucien Carr, who was working as an editor in New York at the time, and asked him for a thousand-dollar advance. Burroughs needed the money: he had sold his land in Texas but hadn't been paid the full amount and what he had wasn't enough to carry out his plan to leave Mexico and go live in another country. Had he written *Junky* mainly for the economic benefit? Maybe not, but that didn't mean he wasn't interested. Throughout his stay in Mexico, he had an ongoing and obvious interest in nailing down a monetary agreement with the potential editor of *Junky*. This is a little-known side of Burroughs, who, like any other gringo entrepreneur in Mexico, made proposals and suggestions, kept accounts, and made calculations about his books, seeing them more as moneymaking opportunities than literary endeavors per se. In equal measure, Burroughs thought of himself as the responsible head of a household, and he had to take precautions. He wrote to Ginsberg:

> Of course, being responsible not only for myself, but also for Joan and the children, I have an absolute duty to place their welfare high on the priority list.

I have not only the right but the duty to carry a gun
and to protect my person against any attack that may de-
prive my family of support. (Ibid., 79)

At the beginning of 1951, Burroughs underwent the Chinese cure, that is, a progressive reduction in heroin dosage
to none at all, and managed to kick in three months. While
he was making superhuman efforts to get off the stuff, one
day a cat stood in his way and he decided to vent all the rage
he'd been experiencing over not shooting up:

There was a cat in the house which we had been feeding,
an ugly-looking gray cat. I picked the animal up and held
it on my lap, petting it. When it tried to jump down I
tightened my hold. The cat began to mew, looking for a
way to escape. I brought my face down to touch the cat's
cold nose with mine, and the cat scratched at my face. It
was a halfassed scratch, and didn't even land. But it was
all I needed. I held the cat out at arm's length, slapping
it back and forth across the face with my free hand. The
cat screamed and clawed me, then started spraying piss
all over my pants. I went on hitting the cat, my hands
bloody from scratches. The animal twisted loose and ran
into the closet, where I could hear it groaning and whim-
pering with terror.

"Now I'll finish the bastard off," I said, picking up a

heavy painted cane. Sweat was running down my face. I was trembling with excitement. I licked my lips and started toward the closet, alert to block any escape attempt. At this point my old lady intervened, and I put down the cane. The cat scrambled out of the closet and ran down the stairs. (Burroughs, *Junky*, 123)

Burroughs included this account in the uncensored version of *Junky*, which, though not the most faithful autobiography, does at times describe just how things happened. Evidently, Joan is the "old lady" who came to the cat's rescue.

THE BOUNTY

Immediately after Burroughs took a break from shooting opiates, he started drinking heavily. He would go to a bar that stood at the base of an apartment building at 122 Calle Monterrey, near the corner of Chihuahua, in the Roma district, called the Bounty (Ship Ahoy in *Queer*). The building was managed by a fortyish, unmarried, short, and dark mestiza: Juanita Peñaloza, a seasoned businesswoman who sublet furnished apartments. Most of the residents were gringos studying at Mexico City College, or said they were, or had jobs in Mexico City. Others were Mexican students who studied art (at La Esmeralda school) or medicine.

As a young woman, Juanita Peñaloza worked at the Hotel Génova, where she met a man who asked her to look after his children abroad. Juanita accepted his offer and spent five years in Europe, where she learned English, French, and Italian. Back in Mexico with the money she'd saved, she started subletting entire buildings, such as the one at 122 Monterrey. Another was at 210 Orizaba, on a residential lane in the Roma district, where Bill and Joan moved shortly afterward. In 1951, Juanita resided with a cousin, Eva, at one of the apartments in the Calle Monterrey building. Like Lola la Chata, Juanita had good business dealings but offered help to those who needed it. She lent money, cared for the sick, and picked people up off the street without asking anything in return.

The American John Healy—together with two compatriots, one of them named Louis Carpio—owned the Bounty. Healy had been a lover to Juanita, who lived in apartment 10. Like Burroughs, Healy didn't like the USA. He had worked in Florida, Nevada, California, Colorado, and Minnesota, and he'd been in the Air Force, but never managed to settle down anywhere. Anyway, he didn't care to work for a wage. One day in Minneapolis he decided to catch the next bus south. He asked the driver what was the furthest he could possibly take him, and the driver responded Mexico City. Healy bought a ticket, recalling what a friend had once told him: for Americans, the first year in Mexico was hellish, but if you stuck it out for a year you wouldn't want to leave.

Shortly after arriving in Mexico City, Healy accepted the offer of a Chinese resident—in fact, the Chinese consul in Mexico City, who felt he should stay there when the communist revolution broke out. He wanted Healy to take over a restaurant that he owned at the storefront of 122 Monterrey in exchange for letting him sell jewelry there. The real name of the place was The Good Ship Bounty, but everyone just called it the Bounty. You could drink and eat there from seven in the morning to eleven at night. Since Mexican laws mandated that drink could only be served accompanied by food, there was a plate of something at each table, so people could drink and eat at the same time. A meal consisting of soup, filet mignon, and dessert cost five pesos.

Like William S. Burroughs, Healy had trouble making his activities legal in Mexico, so he bribed his way through everything. Once he was even deported and had to cross the border, only to come straight back to his apartment at 122 Monterrey. When the police who'd deported him saw that he was back, they told him: "We've done our duty in deporting you. If you want to stick around, that's your problem."

John Healy stayed in Mexico and at the Bounty.

Most of the Bounty's regular customers were gringos. One time a producer for MGM asked Healy if he could find a group of American extras for a picture he was shooting in Mexico City. Healy told his customers and friends from the Bounty that he had some temp work on a film and that the bar would be cleared out for a few days. Everyone went to the set, including Healy himself, who acted alongside William Holden, with whom he got drunk on mezcal, and Stanley Clements. Since Healy's group of friends did whatever they felt like doing, took it easy, disobeyed the director, he fired them. The movie was *Boots Malone*. None of the extras appeared in the final edited version, except Healy who had a very small role.

Healy drank heavily, and, unlike Burroughs, immersed himself in the nightlife of Alemán-era Mexico City. He frequented the Catacumbas and Mil y Una Noches, and knew some well-heeled Mexicans who invited him on all-night— sometimes several-day—Dionysian, alcohol-fueled binges through the capital.

Burroughs checked into the Bounty at five in the afternoon and usually drank vodka or tequila. Healy never actually saw him drunk, except one time—at Burroughs's home after Joan's death. When he went to the Bounty, Burroughs almost always took along Joan and the kids, who played in the street while their parents drank inside the bar. Joan and Bill would sit by the door so they could keep an eye on little Billy and Julie. Forty years later, Healy recalled Joan and the children:

[Joan] drank. I used to drink with her a lot. She would come over for a drinking partner. She didn't like to drink alone. She was an intelligent woman. She was an alcoholic. They'd [Burroughs and Joan] come in and sit around, they always took a table when they were together, they would always take a table near the street, near the sidewalk, then [the two Burroughses'] kids played on the sidewalk, they were good little kids, the boy was kind of hyper, bounced around, couldn't stop bouncing around. But I liked them, they were cute little kids. (Interview with James Grauerholz, unpublished)

On occasion, Joan and Bill would buy a bottle, perhaps of tequila, and if they didn't finish it, they would put a label with their name on it and give it to the bartender to hold on to. The next day they'd request it and drink the remaining contents.

Substituting alcohol for drugs, Burroughs habitually drank to excess. One evening while drinking at another Roma neighborhood bar—possibly the Ku Ku, which was at the corner of Coahuila and Insurgentes and is mentioned in several of Burroughs's and Kerouac's novels—a cop appeared and Burroughs struck up a conversation with him. Suddenly, irked by the man in uniform, Burroughs lost his head, took out a pistol (he never went unarmed while in Mexico City), and pushed it into the policeman's stomach. From behind the bar, the bartender grabbed the arm of the impetuous American, took away his pistol, and checked to see if it was loaded. Burroughs thought of saying, "Of course —what good is an unloaded gun?" but remained silent. The cop took him by the arm, pulled him out to the street, took his gun, and let him go instead of arresting him.

The next morning, Burroughs woke up in a seedy hotel without his wallet, fountain pen, or pocket knife. He checked out of the hotel and went looking for Kells Elvins at his apartment on Ávila Camacho Boulevard. When he got there, he found his friend walking his dog. He drew nearer. Upon seeing Burroughs, a visibly upset Elvins said to him:

You're going to get your head blown off carrying that gun. What do you carry it for? You wouldn't know what you were shooting at. You bumped into trees twice there on Insurgentes. You walked right in front of a car. I pulled you back and you threatened me. I left you there to find your own way home, and I don't know how you ever made it. Everyone is fed up with the way you've been acting lately. If there's one thing I don't want to be around, and I think no one else particularly wants to be around, it's a drunk with a gun. (Burroughs, *Junky*, 132)

Burroughs vaguely recalled this account by Elvins, who, after scolding him, gave him a fifty-dollar bill. Bill went right to the Bounty and drank tequila for the next eight hours straight. He barely managed to get himself home. The next day, he started vomiting. He threw up so much that finally only green bile came out. While he was sprawled on the floor like a dead man, Old Dave showed up. Seeing his friend in such a state, he said, "You got to quit drinking, Bill. You're getting crazy."

Burroughs kept throwing up bile until the afternoon. Then a strong scent pervaded the bedroom and penetrated his nostrils. A smell of piss.

"One of them cats must have pissed under the bed," he murmured.

Old Dave looked over the room. He saw no cats.

"Bill, it's you smells like piss," he told Burroughs, who, holding his nose next to his body, considered what his friend had said, horror-struck.

"Good lord, I got uremic poisoning, go out and get me a croaker," he said to Old Dave, who darted out to find one. In a bit, the Chinese doctor who wrote them scripts for morphine examined Burroughs.

"You don't have uremia, you just have to quit drinking," he said, shrugging his shoulders. Dissatisfied with the diagnosis, Burroughs asked Old Dave to look for Kells Elvins so he could bring his doctor. Later, Old Dave returned with Elvins and the doctor.

The doctor said that Burroughs had only the early signs of uremia. Later, picking up a bottle of tequila that was in the room, he told his patient: "One more of these and you're as good as dead."

Finally, he prescribed an antacid and told him to stop drinking for at least a month. Burroughs took his advice and stopped drinking for a while. After these incidents, he wrote Kerouac: "I was drunk for a month, lost two guns to the Law, and wound up near dying from uremic poisoning. Now I am back on the three cocktail a day schedule" (ibid., 82).

Although he'd stopped shooting heroin and reduced his alcohol intake to three martinis a day, Burroughs smoked opium once a week. He considered the substance harmless. He continued to attend Mexico City College after a fashion, more for the money he got than for any true interest in his studies. He was also revising the manuscript of *Junky*, clearing it of any theoretical references in which he quoted Wilhelm Reich. In a letter to Allen Ginsberg, he argued over the aims of the book:

> Now what in the name of God do you mean by saying the book is a "justification" for junk or myself taking junk? I don't justify nothing to nobody. As a matter of fact, the book is the only accurate account I ever read of the real horror of junk. But I don't mean it as justification or deterrent or anything but an accurate account of what I experienced during the time I was on junk. (Ibid., 83)

Already in early 1951, Burroughs was mentioning in correspondence his desire to expand *Junky* to include a Mexico chapter. This would end up being his second novel, *Queer*, which he wrote as a separate, self-contained text a

few months later. It was never used as the last chapter of
Junky.

Burroughs continued to be disappointed with Mexico,
with its people and, once again, its bureaucracy and police
force. One day in April 1951, there was a forceful knocking
at his door. Still in his pajamas, Burroughs went to open it.
It was an inspector from the immigration department, who
said:

"Get dressed, you're under arrest."

The reason? His papers weren't in order and some neighbors had been complaining about his drunken binges.

"Where's your Mexican wife? Are you a bigamist or
what?" the inspector asked him.

But Burroughs already knew how it was in Mexico,
and after a theatrical quarrel he handed the inspector a
two-hundred-dollar bribe to leave him alone. Everything
pointed toward his leaving Mexico. Time was passing and
the possibility of starting a new business or buying land, or
of becoming a naturalized citizen so he had the right to do
these things, continued to dwindle. Mexico had become impossible, even repugnant:

> Everybody staggering around blind, stupid, sullen, mur-
> derous drunk, but still able to get in there with knives

and machetes and broken bottles and score for three or
four stiffs. And then some cop reels in drunker than any-
body and shoots three or four more people before he re-
alizes he is in the wrong house. (Ibid., 91)

The ambiguity that Burroughs felt toward Mexico seems
quite apparent in the following excerpt from a letter he wrote
to Kerouac in May 1951:

Mexico is not simple or gay or idyllic. It is nothing like a
French-Canadian neighborhood. It is an oriental country
that reflects 2000 years of disease and poverty and degra-
dation and stupidity and slavery and brutality and psy-
chic and physical terrorism. Mexico is sinister and
gloomy and chaotic with the special chaos of a dream. I
like it myself, but it isn't everybody's taste, and don't ex-
pect to find anything like Lowell. . . . No Mexican knows
any other Mexican, and when a Mexican kills someone
(Mexico DF has about the highest murder rate of any city
in the world), it is usually his best friend. I guess they find
a friend less frightening than a stranger. (Ibid.)

How true was the sentence: "I like it myself, but it isn't
everybody's taste"? Had Burroughs just written it to affirm
his irrefutably underground identity? And with Mexico being an underground country compared with the USA, wasn't

it rash of him to write it off or reject it out of hand? The truth was that despite the sordidness and uncivilized behavior of Mexican society, or perhaps because of it, Mexico remained attractive to Burroughs. There existed a certain empathy between the two, a distant but real communicating vessel. That said, Burroughs wanted to get out of Mexico, as he continually stressed in his letters to Ginsberg and Kerouac.

In April of that year, Burroughs wrote an odd letter to his faithful servant Ginsberg; odd more because of Joan's postscript than its contents. In the letter, Burroughs admonished Ginsberg for having slept with a woman for the first time in his life, as if he could overcome his homosexuality in that manner.

> For the Cris sake do you actually think that laying a woman makes someone heterosexual? I have been laying women for the past 15 years and haven't heard any complaints from the women either.* What does that prove except that I was hard up at that time? Laying a woman so far as I am concerned is O.K. if I can't score for a boy. But laying one woman or a thousand merely emphasizes the fact that a woman is not what I want. Better than nothing, of course, like a tortilla is better than no food. But no matter how many tortillas I eat I still want a steak.** (Ibid., 88)

The single and double asterisks in the letter were placed there by Joan; they referred the reader to explanatory comments at the end of the writing. By the first asterisk she wrote: "Correct!" By the second: "Around the 20th of the month, things get a bit a tight and he lives on tortillas." Joan, though conscious and tolerant of Bill's sexual preferences, could not have remained unaffected by them, despite the irony of the situation. What's interesting about the note is that it tells us that Joan and Bill did have sex, at least sporadically.

As he'd stopped using drugs, Burroughs kept away from Dave Tesorero for a spell. Old Dave still owed Burroughs three hundred pesos he'd lent him so he could sell a share of dope and give him back five hundred. Around that time, a former member of the old New York gang showed up in Mexico: Hal Chase, who had arrived in Mexico to study the Zapotec language. Sometimes he and Burroughs went together to a restaurant, the Hollywood Steak House (which they customarily called the Hollywood Stink House), at the corner of Teotihuacán and Insurgentes in the Hipódromo Condesa district, quite close to Roma. It was open all day and night, and some of the key celebrities in Mexico used to go there, such as Silvia Pinal; the young Arturo Durazo, at that time Hugo Olvera's bodyguard; the actress Lupita Torrentera; Adolfo Ruiz Cortines, later to become president; the comedian Loco Valdez; and Bernabé Jurado himself. Burroughs would often go there, sit alone at a table, order something to eat and a cup of coffee, and stay for hours reading an American paper without talking to anyone. Burroughs was attracted to Hal. One time at the Hollywood Steak House, he suggested that he spend the night with him. Hal declined, Burroughs was upset, and from then on they seldom saw each other.

Among Chase's plans while in Mexico was to go to Salina Cruz and build a boat. Before he left, he ran into Joan on the street. Recognizing him, Burroughs's wife moved her head flirtatiously, as she used to do. As he approached her, Hal saw how terribly she had deteriorated, with open sores on her body, frazzled hair, and one arm oddly out of sync with the other. Hal figured that Joan would be unable to climb out of the hole she'd sunken into, though saw that she still held traces of her original beauty. When he was alone, Kerouac and Ginsberg's other buddy felt deeply moved and imagined that Joan really wanted to die.

Now all that Burroughs had left to hope for in Mexico was the money he was owed for his lands in Texas. In May 1951 he wrote to Kerouac: "I don't know how much longer I will be around Mexico City. I am still waiting on my $ from Texas. When I do get that money I will certainly be taking off for points south" (ibid., 93).

While he awaited the moment to leave Mexico, Burroughs continued to go to the Bounty on a regular basis. He met a few Americans there, none of whom had the slightest artistic or intellectual pretensions. One of them was Marvin Apt, from Miami, for whom John Healy organized a going-away party. A day before the event, Healy and Apt were walking down Insurgentes when they spotted the unmistakable silhouette of Burroughs garbed in hat and overcoat. Upon seeing him, they invited him to the party, warning him to come unarmed. Everyone knew Burroughs always carried a piece with him. "Not even a little one?" responded Burroughs. The next day at the party, Healy spotted a small automatic pistol in Burroughs's belt. All he could do was smile.

Another American who was a regular at the Bounty was Arnold Copeland, who had a scholarship to Mexico City College. Burroughs couldn't stand his crudeness. Copeland would belch at any moment and made no attempt to conceal his dislike for Mexicans. "They're so horrible," he said. He always went around with a .25 automatic. One time at the Hollywood Steak House, he came up to the table where Burroughs was drinking and shouted, "You don't know shit—you don't even know what the fucking Boy Scout motto is."

Burroughs took out his .45 automatic, put it on the table and said, "Be prepared."

Another gringo habitué—and co-owner of the Bounty—was Louis Carpio, a crafty Chicano who went back to Chicago soon afterward. He and Burroughs sometimes went to the bullfights together.

A more frequent patron of the Bounty was a young American from Florida, then twenty-one years old: Lewis Marker. At age sixteen he'd enlisted in the army and spent three years in Germany collaborating with the gringo counterintelligence services (during that time J. D. Salinger was doing the same thing in France). Back in Florida and fed up with military discipline, Marker applied for the GI Bill and in 1950 went to study at Mexico City College. In August 1951, Eddie Woods, a childhood friend, with whom he'd played hooky, stolen cars, and disobeyed military orders, caught up with him. In mid-1951, while recovering from a flying accident, Woods, who had remained in the air force since his enlistment at age fifteen, decided to get together with his old friend.

Marker was a gawky, lanky, graceless gringo whose motto in life was "Get rich, sleep till noon, and fuck 'em all." He resided at 122 Monterrey, sharing the apartment with John Healy, Louis Carpio, and an American couple, Glenn and Betty Jones. After arriving in Mexico, Eddie Woods lived in the same flat with these four denizens of the Bounty, where he went quite often to drink rum and Cokes.

In mid-1951, Burroughs met Marker at the Bounty. Quite taken by the scrawny youth, he soon started making moves on an aloof, childish, presumably heterosexual and disdainful Marker. His main tactic was wordplay: the spiel, cooked up and served in small doses, of a thirty-six-year-old man aware of his scant sex appeal, sure of his intellectual superiority to the youth, practically a teenager of twenty-one. The tactic worked: one night, after a few too many rounds and some carefully calculated conversation at the Bounty, Burroughs took Marker to a hotel and made love to him. But Marker didn't care for William S. Burroughs. He slept with him just to do it, not because he was genuinely or irresistibly drawn to him. In contrast, Burroughs was bowled over by Marker. By making love to the youth he could possess his masculinity, which was precisely what he wanted to experience by having sex with another man. Nevertheless, the two did have one thing in common: their detachment from the outside world. Like Burroughs, Marker radiated an air of self-sufficiency and aloofness. Love is blind, but not that blind.

Sleeping with Burroughs meant nothing to Marker, but meant a lot to Burroughs, who felt hurt when his advances on the young man went unrequited. Like any suitor, Burroughs sought any subterfuge possible to be near the object of his affection. One of these was to invite Marker to South America on an all-expenses-paid trip. Marker accepted, so long as he only had to sleep with Burroughs twice a week.

THERE GOES THE NEIGHBORHOOD

Before Burroughs left for South America with Marker, the family moved near to where they had lived for more than a year. Their new home, apartment 8 at 210 Calle Orizaba, was on a residential lane in the Roma district. Still a series of uninhabited plains at the end of the nineteenth century, Roma started filling up with French-style mansions during the Porfirio Díaz regime, built for the aristocracy of the period. Even after the 1910 Mexican Revolution, Roma continued to accommodate the emerging elite, first under Venustiano Carranza, then Álvaro Obregón, who built his own residence on Jalisco Street (later to be named after Obregón himself).

The openly elite character of the Roma district began to fade in the 1920s, and even though it continued to be Mexico City's most respectable neighborhood, the stage was set for its decline. Middle-class dwellings began springing up, coarsening its original aspect. Gradually, Roma was turning into a social and architectural hybrid, particularly in its central and southern sections where Burroughs lived for three years. The area further degenerated in the thirties and forties with the construction of lower-middle-class buildings, apartment complexes, and numerous small businesses, removing any chic or progressive traces that remained.

Not just middle-class Mexicans but Jews, Arabs, Germans, and Spanish émigrés resided in the Roma district during the 1940s. Various celebrities also lived in the neighborhood during the first half of the twentieth century, most of whom Burroughs had never even heard of: the widows of Porfirio Díaz (whose home was on Calle Quintana Roo), Franciso I. Madero, and Álvaro Obregón; the popular singer María Conesa (at the corner of Monterrey and Chiapas), poet Ramón López Velarde (on Avenida Álvaro Obregón), the muralist David Siqueiros, mother Conchita (known as the mastermind behind Obregón's assassination), the painters Remedios Varo and Leonora Carrington (who lived for sixty years, until her death, on Calle de Chihuahua, half a block from 122 Monterrey), the Russian anarchist Victor Serge. The Café de Nadie, which stood on Avenida Álvaro Obregón in the 1920s, was a den of the Stridentist movement, the Mexican version of Dadaism, where Manuel Maples Arce, Arqueles Vela, and Germán List Arzubide, among others, railed against the good behavior and hygiene of Mexican culture. Though, to be sure, Burroughs remained unaware of all that.

The Roma district where Burroughs lived was a middle-class neighborhood rapidly succumbing to commercial development and hardly elitist; it was a tranquil, gray zone of simple architecture and mediocre aesthetics—which didn't seem to matter much to Bill and Joan.

Many years later, their son Billy, who wrote three novels (*Speed*, *Kentucky Ham*, and the unpublished *Prakriti Junction*), recalled his stay in Mexico City in *Kentucky Ham:*

> I have no memory of our flat in the native quarter for reasons soon to become evident, but the spiral staircase that led down from our top floor was banked with cool blue

walls that kept out the heat. . . . At the bottom of the stairs, in poncho and sunlight was my little Mexican friend, Micco, who was the proud possessor of a white rabbit named Chili. I had never worn shoes in my life until one day Chili thumped up to one of my brown and bare toes and bit me like a Gila monster. I went crying to my mother wah!, who was soft and warm and pulsing, and not only got a set of shoes, but also a fresh can of beans. (Burroughs Jr., *Speed/Kentucky Ham*, 194–95)

JUNGLE JOURNEY

Shortly before leaving for South America with Marker, Bill and Joan had a round of the telepathic game they used to play at home. Joan got a piece of paper and wrote down a message while silently transmitting it to Bill: she herself with clouds of smoke hovering around her head and the word *troglodyte* captioning the image.

Spending time with Marker was not Burroughs's only reason for going to South America. He was also in search of two things: a place where he could achieve what he'd been unable to in Mexico; and *yagé*, the psychoactive Amazonian plant that supposedly possessed telepathic powers. He'd

first heard mention of the substance in the American maga-
zine *Argosy*. Soon after Burroughs and Marker departed for
South America, Joan wrote Ginsberg:

> Bill has taken off for Panama and possibly Ecuador, in
> company with a pretty boy from school. . . . He and the
> kid are going to look over prospects down there, and if
> they find anything that looks good the children and I will
> go on down. I think they're going to Panama City, and if
> that turns out to be too expensive, they'll go to Ecuador
> and maybe even Peru. We like Mexico, but Gobernación
> apparently doesn't like us—one damn fine after another,
> no prospects of getting any papers, no possibility of any
> job or investment. (Quoted in Morgan, *Literary Outlaw*,
> 188)

As Joan was making the same assessment of Mexico that
Bill had and tolerating her husband's running off to South
America with a pretty boy, Bill and Marker were flying to
Panama. There they visited a cabaret, the Blue Goose,
which Burroughs had read in *Argosy* was a spectacular center for drug trafficking. In reality, the Goose was no more
than a cheesy bar without the slightest charm.

Marker figured that Burroughs was fond of fantasizing
about things and assumed his *yagé* expedition would turn
out similarly.

From Panama they flew to Quito. There Burroughs fell ill, perhaps because of the altitude and chilly air of the Andes. One night, sleeping in the same room (but not the same bed) as Marker, he dreamed that he was in a jail surrounded by high mountains, then left the room to take a stroll. While he was walking down a dirty, cobblestone street, an icy mountain wind whipped past him. At that moment, he awoke, tightened the strap on his leather jacket, and felt a chill of desperation.

From Quito they went to the port of Manta, where they stayed at the Hotel Continental. Trouble arose when Burroughs demanded more sex with Marker than they'd agreed on. Marker stuck to their original agreement; despite all the cunning arguments that Burroughs devised, the handsome lad not only refused to yield but felt disgusted by Burroughs's insistence. The overabundance of statues commemorating Simón Bolívar throughout Manta prompted Burroughs to refer to the South American hero as that "liberating fool."

While they were in Manta, avid adventurer if clueless navigator Burroughs thought about buying a boat and returning to Mexico along the Pacific Coast. A prohibition on selling boats to foreigners prevented the trip from happening. Almost forty years later, Marker commented that had they purchased the boat, American literature would have been deprived of one of its most prominent figures.

But his lust for adventure did not end there. Burroughs found out about an American botanist, Dr. Fuller, who lived with the Indians in the middle of the jungle near the Peruvian border and knew about or studied *yagé*. Unable to resist, he convinced Marker to go to the jungle with him. With the unenthusiastic youth in tow, he went questing after the miraculous substance. For the first time in his life, Burroughs conceived of a drug not as simply a way to conquer boredom or succumb to an uncontrollable addiction but as a consciousness expander and catalyst.

Burroughs and Marker caught a rudimentary, jury-rigged bus, a two-and-a-half-ton vehicle with wooden planks as seats. After a tortuous, syncopated fourteen-hour journey, in which Marker complained more than Burroughs, they arrived in Puyo, where the jungle began. It was raining hard. Marker wanted to rest, but Burroughs insisted they keep on without stopping. Along the way, Burroughs would not let Marker pause, even for an instant.

"If you rest, your legs get stiff," he told the exhausted youth.

It was amid adversity that Burroughs always excelled; smooth going failed to inspire or aid him. Several hours later, they arrived at the home of the aforementioned doctor, a thin, older man who lived with his wife, a redheaded former nurse. To Marker, Dr. Fuller seemed like a mad scientist who'd discovered the medical properties of curare, a substance that served as both a muscle relaxant and monkey poison. His discoveries had been filched by one of his assistants, who published the doctor's findings under his own name.

At first, Fuller acted friendly toward his visitors, but when he found out that they weren't planning to leave, his attitude suddenly shifted and he turned distrustful. In his chat with the doctor, Burroughs found out that he was well treated by the indigenous people of the region, because he had once saved the life of one of the chief's daughters. Then Burroughs brought up his interest in *yagé*, but Fuller avoided the subject and did not bring it up again.

That night the visitors slept on the porch. While they were trying to sleep, Fuller burst out of the house; he'd heard a certain frog croaking and went after it to perform some lab experiments. That night Burroughs dreamed he was in front of the Bounty and that suddenly he heard his son Billy crying. He took him in his arms, and when the boy fell silent, it was Burroughs who began to cry. Around him were people dressed in prison suits who could not understand what he was doing there. As it became obvious that Fuller was not going to help him find *yagé*, Burroughs and Marker left the next day. They went back to Quito, continued through Panama, and by September arrived back in Mexico City.

UNDER THE VOLCANO

While Burroughs and Marker were roaming around South America and penetrating the lush jungles of the Amazon basin, Allen Ginsberg and Lucien Carr were on their way from New York to Mexico City in a beat-up old Chevrolet to visit Joan. In mid-August they knocked at the door of apartment 8, at 210 Orizaba. Joan was alone at home with seven-year-old Julie and Billy, who'd just turned four.

After several years of not seeing Joan, Ginsberg saw that she had deteriorated, withered. "She'll be giving you competition soon," he told her upon noticing the girl's blossoming beauty. "Oh, I'm out of the running," responded Joan, looking out the corner of her eye at the bottle of tequila that stood on the table. Afterward, they all had *huevos rancheros*. Ginsberg and Lucien were surprised by Joan's indifference—feigned—toward Bill's absence. She hardly mentioned him in their chats.

Lucien and Joan understood each other well from the first, perhaps because of their mutual penchant for alcohol. One day they went to the Bounty. While they were drinking Oso Negro gin and Coca-Cola, Joan recognized the tune that the jukebox was playing—"El cobarde" (The coward), by Pedro Infante—as a couple of drunken youths stood beside it.

"I think they put it on to provoke you," Joan told Lucien. Later they played "El borracho" (The drunk) and Joan commented to her now-soused companion: "I think that because of your alcoholic consumption, you have now been accepted."

"Well, that's something of an improvement," responded Lucien as he raised his glass for a toast.

A week of no-holds-barred drinking ensued. Lucien, who had come to Mexico to attend a friend's wedding, ended up so drunk that when he took the newlyweds to the airport in his Chevy the police threw him in jail for a night. The next day, Joan suggested they go to Guadalajara, where she said she had a marijuana connection. Everyone, including the kids, piled into the Chevy, and they took the highway to the Bajío region. A smashed Lucien drove recklessly, egged on by Joan, hungry for kicks. Noting the inability of the driver to control the pedals, Joan would crouch down from time to time and handle them as best she could. In the rear, meanwhile, the cowering children shrieked with fear, and Ginsberg scolded Lucien, to no avail. Lucien and Joan went on roaring with laughter. In his previously cited novel, Billy Burroughs penned his recollections of this trip:

> I had a half sister named Julie, full of smiles—a tiny naked dancer who was my mother's daughter. She was only two years older than I, and the first hint of disaster that I can recall was an impossible mad drive along whimsically sudden changing mountain roads, terrifying glimpses of death rusting wreckage far below and hearing my mother saying, "Ha *ha*, how fast can this old heap go?" Julie and I spent the trip on the floor of the back in the intimacy of fear as Allen pleaded with the driver to slow down. Finally we hit something and there was a little blood, but not much. (Burroughs Jr., *Speed/Kentucky Ham*, 195)

They spent the night in the car, by the banks of Lake Chapala, where twenty years earlier D. H. Lawrence had been inspired to write his Aztec novel *The Plumed Serpent*.

From Guadalajara they went to the state of Michoacán, where the recently born Paracutín volcano was erupting. Joan and Lucien continued to drink and carry on together. Observing them from a distance, Ginsberg was pleased to see how they bonded. Everyone spent a night in the car, which was parked at the edge of a precipice that the volcano had made. Later on they stayed at a hotel near a river, where Joan and Lucien had a drunken, giddy swim. All of which led Ginsberg to surmise that the two shared the same bed that night.

After a week's vacation in central Mexico, Joan, kids, and friends went back home. It was late August. Burroughs had not returned, and Lucien and Ginsberg climbed into the Chevy, a reminder of Neal Cassady's epic cars, and headed back to the United States. The affair between Joan and Lucien—if that is in fact what it was—remained there. Ginsberg said that during the return trip, Lucien told him that he'd thought of asking Joan to come along with them to New York. But he didn't do it, thinking it inappropriate to make off with his friend's wife.

The trip to South America had been a fiasco for Burroughs. Rather than bringing him closer to Marker, the relationship went cold and became an annoyance to the younger man. The search for new land had proved fruitless and the *yagé* experience led nowhere. Burroughs returned to Mexico without achieving anything he had set out to do, feeling frustrated, with a heavy heart and an unpaid debt to destiny. By early September Bill and Joan were together again.

THE STRAY BULLET

At noon on Thursday, September 6, 1951, William S. Burroughs heard the whistle of the roving knife sharpener outside his house. As he'd purchased a vintage Scout knife with metal handle in Ecuador, he decided to visit the sharpener. Almost thirty-five years later, in the introduction to *Queer*, Burroughs recalled:

> The knife-sharpener had a little whistle and a fixed route, and as I walked down the street towards his cart a feeling of loss and sadness that had weighed on me all day so I could hardly breathe intensified to such an extent that I found tears streaming down my face.
>
> "What on earth is wrong?" I wondered. (Burroughs, *Queer*, xxi)

Burroughs went back home and began drinking. Around 3:30 p.m., he picked up a bag, put a pistol into it, and went out with Joan in the direction of John Healy's apartment, No. 10, 122 Monterrey. The kids stayed at the neighbors'. In need of cash, Burroughs apparently had an appointment with an American acquaintance (Marvin Apt or Allison, an American who lived at 122 Monterrey) interested in buying one of his guns. According to John Healy, the appointment was made up; neither Apt nor Allison, nor anyone else, wanted to purchase a weapon: Burroughs and Joan were simply going to have a few drinks at their friends' apartment.

Already at the apartment when they arrived were Healy, Marker, his friend Eddie Woods—who at that time was living at Healy's place and was not favorably impressed by Burroughs—and, according to Healy, possibly Betty Jones, an American habitué of the Bounty, a friend and possibly lover of Marker, who also resided at the apartment. Empty bottles of gin and soft drinks littered the flat, a sure sign that the party had been going on for some time. A few days earlier, several Mexico City College students had received their monthly stipend and, as was the custom, blown it on a binge.

Joan and Bill poured themselves Oso Negro gin with lemonade. Very soon afterward, Healy left to go downtown and see Glenn Jones, Betty's husband, who had broken his leg (Glenn and Betty were separated). The others stuck around: Joan, Marker, Woods, and perhaps Betty Jones, chattering away and drinking in a state of apparent calm. Joan showed no signs of jealousy, nor did Marker sense any tension.

Burroughs took a Star .380 automatic pistol, loaded, from his bag, put it on the table beside him, and sat across from Joan, who had settled into a battered chair. Marker and Woods sat on a sofa by her side.

Around two hours after his arrival, William Seward Burroughs turned to Marker and Woods, telling them of his desire to move the family someplace near a certain river in South America where, because of the tides, you could only get there but couldn't leave, so they would live by hunting wild animals. With a sneer on her lips, Joan responded that they'd probably die of hunger.

"Joanie, let me show the boys what a great shot old Bill is," Burroughs responded. "I guess it's about time for our William Tell act."

And, rising from the chair, he stretched out his hand and grabbed the pistol from the table. Joan promptly got up, picked up a half-full glass—a small one—and placed it on her head. As she did this, she closed her eyes, and said with a choked laugh, "I can't watch this—you know I can't stand the sight of blood."

Witnessing such an unexpected scene, Marker didn't make much of it. He figured that if Joan was willing to consent to such a frightful game, it was because of her inherent trust in her husband's marksmanship. Woods, however, found the situation ridiculous. How were they going to explain the inevitable hole in the wall to Juanita Peñaloza, not to mention the numerous shards of glass that would scatter all over the place? He was about to pick up the weapon while it was still near him on the table, but then he thought that doing so would only make matters worse and he held off. Burroughs stood at a distance of three meters from Joan. He noticed that her eyes were shut. He aimed at the glass and pulled the trigger. At that very moment—as he was to discover years later—an addiction to writing penetrated his body.

Joan fell to the floor. At first, everyone—especially the shooter—thought she was kidding and waited a few seconds for Joan's reaction. But when Marker observed the trickle of blood on the floor, the intact glass rolling in circles on the tile, and heard a strange rattle emitting from Joan, he realized that Bill's aim had failed. At first, all he thought of was to get away and have nothing else to do with the matter. But then he thought better of it and, before running off in search of the medical student who lived on the roof, said to Burroughs: "Bill, I think you hit her."

Only after hearing these words and detecting the thin stream of blood trickling down his wife's temple to the floor did Burroughs realize what had happened. He threw himself compulsively at Joan and began shouting her name desperately, begging her to speak. Woods left Burroughs kneeling and sobbing beside Joan's body and went to the apartment of Juanita Peñaloza, who quickly phoned the Red Cross, the police, and Bernabé Jurado. As soon as she hung up, she told Woods and Marker the instructions that Jurado had given her: as they were considered the only witnesses, they should stay at a hotel and talk to him that night so he could tell them what to do.

The ambulance reached the Red Cross at 7:30 p.m. Still alive, Joan was taken to the emergency room. The doctors performed blood transfusions, fed her oxygen and serum, and did everything they could to save her. All in vain: Joan died an hour after her arrival at the hospital. The police standing guard outside could no longer question her. The cadaver spent the night in the Red Cross auditorium. No one kept watch over Joan that night, nor did anyone claim her body. The next day, it was transported to Juárez Hospital, where an autopsy was done.

Meanwhile, as Healy tells it, the police and reporters entered the scene of the crime, where they piled up and straightened the empty soft drink and Oso Negro gin bottles, the overflowing ashtrays, half-full glasses, and the pistol that Burroughs had fired, then added more bottles to the pile (some Las Glorias de Cuba rum). When the scene was ready, they took photos and made their respective investigations.

THE TRIAL

When John Healy showed up at this apartment, he was so nervous that, according to press reports, he said that Joan had arrived at the flat twenty minutes before Bill, to visit John Herrman (a mutual American friend who lived in Guadalajara but was at that time in Mexico City). In fact, Herrman was quite a ways from the scene of the incidents. Healy laughed uneasily each time the police asked him something, saying he didn't understand a word of Spanish. Actually, he was scared to death. That same day, Herrman denied what Healy had said. These statements were presented by the press as irrefutable proof that Joan's killing was a crime of passion and that most probably Burroughs had killed her out of jealousy of Healy or Herrman.

The first statement that Burroughs made at the police desk inside the Red Cross hospital, where Joan had been taken before her death, stuck to the truth: she had placed a glass of gin on her head so that he could shoot it with a pistol. The shot missed and lodged in his wife's temple. But right after Joan died, Jurado arrived at the Red Cross and, when they were alone, he told Burroughs to change his statement and to say that, after having one too many, he examined his pistol. He dropped it and it went off, and that's how

Joan had been wounded. This is what he said at the Eighth Precinct. The press would not forgive him, though, and the next day in the country's top papers the highly sellable news appeared, over eight columns, that Burroughs, extremely drunk and feeling like William Tell, had killed his wife with a single bullet, and only afterward in passing did they mention his second statement. All in all, Jurado's swift, opportune, and shrewd intervention set the course for the developments that followed.

When Burroughs was told at the Red Cross that Joan had died, he began wailing disconsolately, tearing at his hair, without being able or wanting to conceal his desperation. Later on, Burroughs made his statement at the Eighth Precinct. He was then taken to the penitentiary known as the Black Palace of Lecumberri.

In the days that followed, Burroughs again denied emulating William Tell and, on Jurado's urging, he stood by his statement that the shot that killed Joan was the result of his accidentally dropping the pistol, though he added certain nuances suggested by Jurado, who was thinking of the ballistics experts. To that end, the fastest attorney in the Mexican West had already spoken with Marker, Woods, and Healy, advising them exactly what to do and say both inside and outside the courtroom.

A short time before he made his statement at the district attorney's office, Marker met with Burroughs at the prison. Burroughs told him to go to the house at 210-8 Calle Orizaba and remove anything that might incriminate him with the police. Marker went to the Bounty to look for John Healy, and both of them headed for Burroughs's place. Healy recalls what happened:

Then I went to the Bounty and met Marker and he says to me "Jeez, Johnny, Bill wants us to go to his apartment and get rid of anything he's got up there, there are some syringes and stuff, get it out of there, not that it means anything, but they don't want a bad impression." So Marker and I went there, but we couldn't go in the front door because there were squad cars out there, so we went around, we walked back, pretended we didn't even see them, and we went to another building and we climbed up the back of the building and got over to the patio and got into Bill's place. We got in there, and there was a pipe in there—he smoked weed, a concrete material, maybe ceramic—we got that and we got some Mary, and we got some syringes and anything like that. We just put it in a package and climbed out the way we did [came in]. Then we went to a theater in the neighborhood and we walked down and went in and dumped all this stuff into a trash thing there. And that was it. (Interview with James Grauerholz, unpublished)

Three days after Burroughs's arrest—and official orders he be sent to prison—Marker, Woods, Healy, and Betty Jones made their statements to the judge, Eduardo Urzaiz Jiménez, and the prosecutor, Rogelio Barriga Rivas, author of several realist novels. Burroughs himself was present. Healy and Jones were considered non-eyewitnesses even though, as has already been mentioned, Healy said that Jones was possibly inside the apartment when Burroughs shot Joan, a point that Jurado, the accused, and the other two eyewitnesses took great pains to conceal.

The plan cooked up by Jurado worked. The witnesses' statements gibed with Burroughs's version in saying that Joan's death was an accident and that Burroughs never meant to kill her. Bernabé Jurado thus played the card of gaining his client's conditional release and postponement of the definitive trial for one year. Burroughs would be released on bail for a year until his definitive sentence was determined.

Four days after Joan died, Mortimer Burroughs, Bill's

older brother, arrived in Mexico City from St. Louis. Decorous, conventional, well-mannered, opposed to his brother's way of life and thought, Mortimer went to Mexico to post $2,312 bail to the Mexican courts and $2,300 to Jurado for his services—$300 of which went to bribe the ballistics experts—and to arrange Billy's return to the United States.

After easily handling the trial and bribing the experts, Jurado resolved the case in his client's favor, and Burroughs left prison on bail, obliged to provide his signature each Monday at the courthouse until he was sentenced. Burroughs spent thirteen days at Lecumberri. Considering the seriousness of the case, it was a record release time for Jurado. Burroughs's time in a Mexican prison was not all that harsh. Rather than harassing him for the crime they charged him for, people helped him in many ways, as he wrote in a letter to Ginsberg:

> While sojourning in the box, I was greatly impressed by the kindness and decency of the Mexican people. Can you imagine during my preliminary interrogation at the precinct the cops were telling me what to say. "You must deny that. You must say this." And in prison a man gave me one of his two blankets, and believe me it is cold in there at night sleeping on a slab of tin. (Harris, *The Letters of William S. Burroughs*, 98)

Out of jail, Burroughs went to meet Mortimer at the Hotel Reforma, where he was staying. Burroughs spent the night with his brother. Their encounter was unusual. For the first time in either of their lives, they opened up to one another. They wept, drank, talked about the family, about themselves, they confessed their old secrets and feelings. Burroughs acknowledged with some guilt that he'd failed to do his part in attending to family matters. The two would never again be together like this. Mortimer died in St. Louis in 1981, a month before Billy Burroughs.

At the time Burroughs shot Joan, Billy and Julie were staying with the neighbors. It is highly likely that until Mortimer's arrival, no one except the neighbors took care of the children. Before Burroughs left prison, Joan's parents arrived in Mexico. They wanted to take their grandchildren to their home in Albany. After his release, Burroughs met them at the American consulate. No violent clash ensued when the three came face-to-face, though Joan's mother could hardly conceal the scorn she felt toward the author for the death of her daughter. At the same time, Burroughs felt no sense of obligation toward Joan's progenitors, who had helped their daughter very little and with whom they had never had a close relationship, not even an epistolary one.

On the ninth of September, Joan was buried in grave 1018-A at the American Cemetery, located at México-Tacuba Avenue in Mexico City. Only dirt marked the space where she was inhumed: no stone, no inscription, nothing with her name on it. Mortimer Burroughs handled the paperwork and expenses for the burial. Because of the apparent abandonment of the grave and the absence of relatives or acquaintances to take care of it, in January 1993 the cemetery authorities decided to remove Joan's cadaver, put the remains in a bag, and place it in a niche at the far side of the cemetery: No. 82, class R, section PR. Before they chose to do this, they published a notification in the *Diario Oficial de México* (the public record), calling on relatives of the slain woman to come forth and claim the remains in the original grave and request they not be moved. No one responded to the call.

Joan's parents took Julie and Billy to the United States. But before they left for Albany—as they'd agreed on with Burroughs—they stopped in St. Louis to pay a visit to Burroughs's parents and see if they would take custody of Billy. When Laura Lee Burroughs told Joan's parents that Billy would stay in St. Louis with them, Joan's mother could not contain herself and railed against William S. Burroughs: "I hope Bill Burroughs goes to hell and stays there."

Julie grew up in Albany with her grandparents. Years later she married in New York State, where she's lived ever since. When Billy died in 1981, Julie was sent a letter notifying her of the burial date. She didn't even respond. In the mid-1980s, one of Burroughs's biographers, Ted Morgan, wrote her to request an interview. Julie declined on the basis that she remembered nothing of her childhood before she went to live with her grandparents.

Billy was raised by his paternal grandparents and from a very young age followed in his father's footsteps, consuming drugs and alcohol in abundant quantities and writing about his experiences with them. At age twenty-nine, he had a liver transplant. Four and a half years later he died in Florida. He inherited his father's self-destructiveness, if not invulnerability, and his mother's fragility.

My mother (Joan was her name) was not one of reason and she had soft brown hair and heart-shaped calves seen from behind. Some time later, my grandmother spoke to me in a failing voice about how timid Joan had been in "correct" company (meaning herself, poor doll), and how she spoke only to Bill . . .

So mama was tempestuous to say the least, and one night at a party in our home where everyone was plastered or stoned, she placed an apple or an apricot or a grape or myself on her head and challenged my father to shoot. Bill, usually an excellent marksman, missed. . . . So I can remember no details of the apartment, or my mother.

. . . one New York cold Chinatown night [Allen Ginsberg] told me that my mother was also a death freak as is anyone who makes a habit of speed. He said he had the morgue photograph if I wanted to see it, but I chuckled chilly uneasy and said something to the effect of "maybe later." (Burroughs Jr., *Speed/Kentucky Ham*, 195–96)

THE UGLY SPIRIT

Over the course of his life, Burroughs interpreted Joan's death in different ways. Similarly, his public statements on the matter have sometimes varied. For quite some time he referred to it as a simple accident, as an undesirable or unfortunate incident, and avoided speaking much about it, downplaying it or remaining completely mum. In his books where Mexico plays a key role—*Junky* and *Queer*—he never utters a word about it. Until 1985, he referred to Joan's death only in general terms, reiterating the deceitful statement that Bernabé Jurado had instructed him to tell the Mexican courts, denying anything about a round of William Tell, without ever going into it in depth. In an interview with *Paris Review* in 1965, for example, he stated:

> And I had that terrible accident with Joan Vollmer, my wife. I had a revolver that I was planning to sell to a friend. I was checking it over and it went off—killed her. A rumor started that I was trying to shoot a glass of champagne from her head William Tell style. Absurd and false.

Only thirty-five years after it occurred did he come clean with a coherent, in-depth interpretation of what happened. In 1985, Burroughs decided to publish his novel *Queer*, written entirely in Mexico, which he'd kept in his drawer for exactly thirty-five years. In an extensive preface to the book, he expounded on his vision of Mexico and his interpretation of Joan's death. This introduction lifted the veil that had for so long remained drawn. Burroughs's response to the event is surprising, perhaps as much for the time transpired as for its content.

Joan's death was a great revelation (or antirevelation) to Burroughs, the experience that determined the course of his life ever since, in particular as a writer, but not just that. It was the harbinger of a reality that was as unavoidable as it was terrifying; in short, the appearance in his life, for the first time, of an "Ugly Spirit." What is meant by this is an "exogenous" power whose energy has the clear objective of possessing and taking hold of possessable subjects. According to Burroughs, it was this spirit that made him fire the pistol and took control of him from that point on. This was the interpretation provided by Brion Gysin (his teacher and friend, who passed away in 1986) at the Beat Hotel in Paris in the late 1950s.

> "Ugly spirit shot Joan to be cause," that is, to maintain a hateful parasitic occupation. My concept of possession is closer to the medieval model than to modern psychological explanation, with their dogmatic insistence that such manifestations must come from within and never, never, never, from without. (As if there were some clear clear-cut difference between inner and outer.) . . . This occasion was my first clear indication of something in my being that was not me, and not under my control. (Burroughs, *Queer*, xix)

The obsessions that plagued Burroughs from then on can be traced to this revelation. The Ugly Spirit was to become the source of inspiration for the essential elements in his work and life—viruses, control, forces of destruction—but also for their counterpart, the ways of liberating oneself from their presence. In fact, the death of Joan—which is to say, his own death—made Burroughs a writer, a terminal writer, a writer who could not survive without writing. The act of writing was his only weapon, the only antidote he had to attenuate this possession, to withstand and endure it.

I am forced to the appalling conclusion that I would never have become a writer but for Joan's death, and to a realization of the extent to which this event has motivated and formulated my writing. I live with the constant threat of possession, and a constant need to escape from possession, from Control. So the death of Joan brought me in contact with the invader, the Ugly Spirit, and maneuvered me into a lifelong struggle, in which I have had no choice except to write my way out. (Ibid., xxii)

This is Burroughs's take; there are others. It could be said, for example, that his misogyny exploded at that moment; that his hatred for familial convention made him pull the trigger of his Star .380, inasmuch as Joan represented family responsibilities; that the shot was a hysterical affirmation of his homosexuality, barely satisfied at that time; that it was a demonstration of his love for Marker; or that a tawdry spirit did in fact possess him and forced him to propel the bullet into Joan's temple.

That said, what is notable about Burroughs's interpretation is the utter absence of any reference to the obviously self-destructive personality and dynamic of Joan. One reading that makes some sense is that Burroughs killed his wife because she wanted to die, and that, capitalizing on a magnificent alternative to committing suicide, she agreed under the circumstances (Burroughs was bewildered after his trip to South America, Marker was present, Joan herself felt frustrated at her inability to start something with Lucien Carr) to place the gin glass on her head and fervently wished that the bullet would penetrate her forehead, or else ordered Burroughs (in the manner of their telepathic games) to miss the glass but not her head. There are countless versions. Beyond the accuracy of the interpretations, Joan's death served two purposes: so Joan could finally achieve her mission of dying and so Burroughs could give the world an oeuvre of immeasurable visionary value. Undoubtedly, Joan did not separate from Burroughs because she saw him as an emissary of her death, and Burroughs would not have been able to think, write, or paint as he thought, wrote, and painted without having gone through the terrible experience of Joan's death. The couple had a reciprocal relationship. Burroughs gave Joan her passport to another life. Joan opened an unsuspected door for Burroughs, without which

William S. Burroughs at the Octava Delegación, the office where suspects were placed immediately following arrest, before his transfer to Palacio de Lecumberri prison, September 6, 1951.

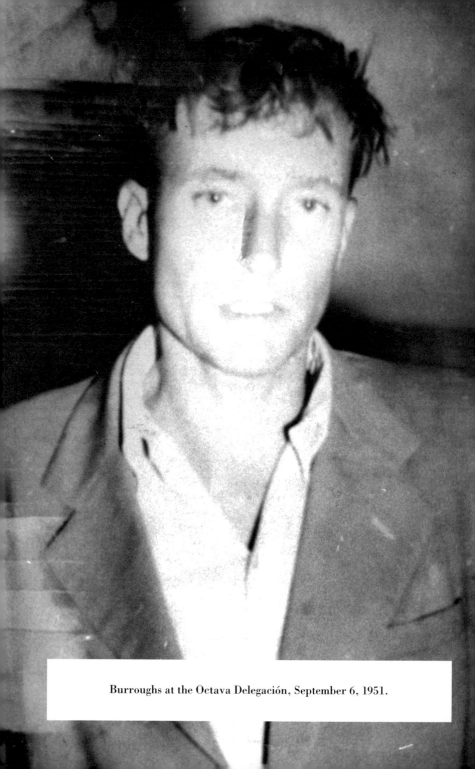

Burroughs at the Octava Delegación, September 6, 1951.

Burroughs at the Octava Delegación, September 6, 1951.

John Healy, owner of the Bounty bar, and Juanita Peñaloza, subletter
of the building at 122 Calle Monterrey, during Burroughs's trial at the
Octava Delegación, September 7, 1951.

Eddie Woods and Lewis Marker, friends of Burroughs and witnesses to the shooting of Joan Vollmer, at the Octava Delegación, September 7, 1951.

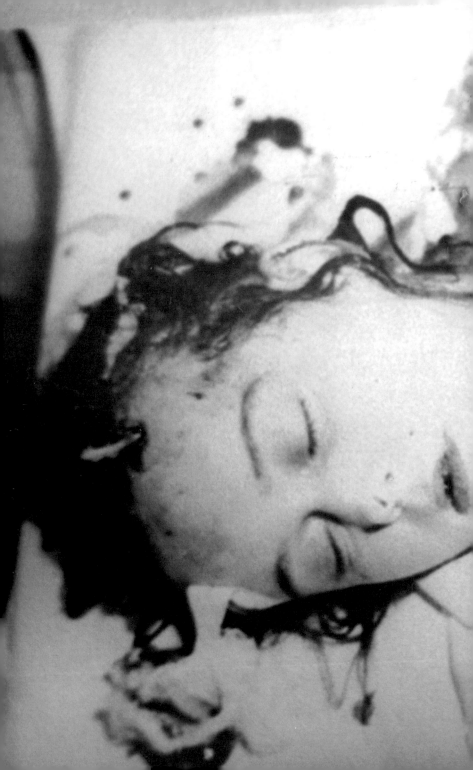

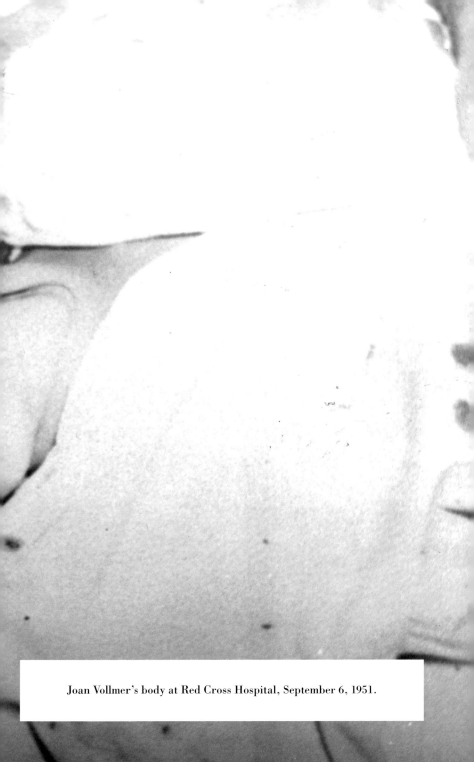

Joan Vollmer's body at Red Cross Hospital, September 6, 1951.

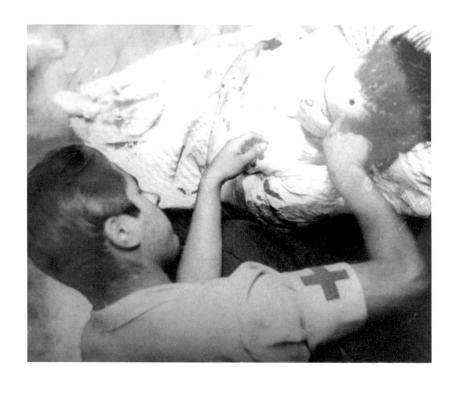

Attendant with Joan Vollmer's body at Red Cross Hospital, September 6, 1951.

he would never have been able to see or create as he did. The gods know how to run this world.

A few days after Allen Ginsberg and Lucien Carr left Mexico, Carr's dilapidated Chevrolet broke down in Galveston, Texas. Lucien caught a plane to New York, intending to return in a week with money. Ginsberg waited for him in a seedy hotel in Galveston; the Chevy sat in the parking lot. Two days later, browsing a newspaper, Allen read the news of Joan's death. He was stunned. Memories paraded through his head: the days when he first met Bill and Joan in New York, his and Kerouac's desire to bring them together, and the recent trip to Mexico where he spent time with a greatly deteriorated and unhinged Joan, eager for alcohol-fueled, out-on-a-limb experiences, her soul in disarray, without anywhere to get a foothold. Perhaps his friend's death did not come as much of a surprise. He even thought that Joan had somehow brought on her own death. Two days later, he wrote a letter from Galveston to Carolyn Cassady, Neal's wife, who lived in San Francisco and who, like her husband, had already seen in the newspaper what had happened in Mexico: "Lucien and Joan played games of chance with drunken driving, egging each other on suicidally at times, while we were there. . . . My imagination of the scene and psyches in Mexico is too limited to comprehend the past misery and absurdity and sense of drama that must exist in Bill's mind now" (Cassady, *Off the Road*, 151).

MONDAY, SIGNATURE DAY

After Burroughs got out of jail, he was obliged to stay in Mexico City until the definitive judgment was made on the charges against him. Burroughs was legally classified as a "pernicious foreigner," and had to sign his name every Monday for his conditional freedom. He went back to living at 210 Orizaba, but this time, so as not to stir up memories, he moved to apartment 5 (previously he had lived with his family in number 8). He was now alone, without Joan, without the kids. He held the illusory belief that the trial would take place quite soon, in perhaps a few weeks' time, and so he was prepared to leave Mexico at any moment. Shortly after leaving Lecumberri, he wrote Ginsberg:

> My case is still pending, but the lawyer [Bernabé Jurado] assures me there will be no further difficulty. When Kells [Elvins] asked him if there was any possibility of me going back to the joint, he says real shocked: "What! Mr. Burroughs go back to prison? Do you think I want to jeop-

ardize my reputation as a lawyer?" You see he got me out in record time for a homicide case, so I am a sample of his work. Every time I see him he buys me drinks and calls all his prospective clients over to look at me. "There he is! Thirteen days! Nobody else in Mexico could have done it in that time!" (Harris, *The Letters of William S. Burroughs*, 95)

Burroughs was impressed by Jurado's meteoric and efficient work, by his personality and ability to maneuver. What to do now? What but write, revise *Junky*, write *Queer*, and continue obsessing over Marker without being requited, despite Burroughs's efforts to deepen their relationship. When the scrawny youth fell ill with jaundice in December 1951, Burroughs moved over to his apartment and nursed him back to health, but even this did not gain Marker's love or affection. On the contrary, Marker no longer wanted an intimate relationship with Burroughs. Even though he admired, respected, and valued him, he drew the line at sex.

These are the subjects most often discussed in Burroughs's letters to Ginsberg and Kerouac during this period: his writing, chiefly with regard to revisions, publication and sales of *Junky*, the preparation of *Queer*, and his impossible love for Marker, who, unfortunately for Burroughs, traveled to Oklahoma to visit his grandmother at the beginning of 1952 and did not return until September. In his correspondence to Ginsberg during those months, Burroughs spoke of Marker as his "boy" in an attempt to portray his relationship with the standoffish young man as stable and harmonic, which was utterly false. Despite Marker's patent rejection, he provided a necessary illusion for Burroughs, an indispensable fantasy to resort to in his moments of anxiety, a way to fill the emptiness he felt because of Joan's death.

Burroughs now entered the bleakest phase of his stay in Mexico, a tunnel of shadows, woe, and disillusion—much like the tone of the book he was writing at that time, *Queer*. By November 1951, he was only sporadically using drugs: a sudden syringe of heroin, a bit of opium in his coffee, and marijuana. (After his visit to Panama, that country's grass seemed far superior to any other's.) But by February 1952 he was shooting up at least once a day, while trying to reduce the habit with a tincture of opium and codeine, the latter purchased without a prescription at Mexican pharmacies.

Burroughs still wanted to go to South America to buy arable land and be self-sufficient and even conduct business. Ecuador was his country of choice. Now added to his wish to acquire a farm was a renewed desire to try *yagé*

(*Banisteriopsis caapi*, or ayahuasca), revealer of ultimate truths, as noted in the final sentence of *Junky:* "Maybe I will find in yage what I was looking for in junk and weed and coke. Yage may be the final fix" (Burroughs, *Junky*, 95).

QUEER

In late March 1952, Burroughs was working nonstop on what he was calling at the time the second part of *Junky*, later *Queer*. Although Burroughs conceived of this book as a complement to the first, the differences between the two are obvious and informed—as he would recognize thirty-five years later—by Joan's death. *Junky*, written in the first person, is a candid account of Burroughs's experience with drugs. Delivered in a cold, direct style, it was free of any drama or sense of personal tragedy. *Queer*, written in the third person, relates one segment of Burroughs's homosexual experiences in Mexico, centered on the impossibility of his relationship with Marker. In *Queer*, Lee, the main character who happens to have the same name as *Junky*'s central figure, displays the loneliness and angst that Burroughs felt immediately after Joan's death. The tone is more intimate, even in the absence of any tragedy.

In *Queer*, the events being narrated bear an existential burden that is missing in *Junky*. Thirty-five years later, in a new introduction to the book, Burroughs confessed that he felt chills rereading the manuscript after so many years. The drama in *Queer* comes more from the author who wrote it than from what he wrote. Far from openly facing the harsh fact of Joan's death and expressing it in the novel, he consciously avoids it by removing any reference to the disgraceful event, or even to the existence of his wife. Joan never appears in the novel.

If there exists a "Mexican novel" in Burroughs's oeuvre, *Queer* is it. Not because Mexico takes the foreground but because the main character's drama has this country as a stage, even if it is a vague and distant one. In *Queer* there is little concern for sketching a portrait of Mexico at that point in time. It's a short novel that relates the devastating experiences of a foreigner on Mexican soil. In this it is akin to *Under the Volcano* by Malcolm Lowry or *The Power and the Glory* by Graham Greene. Like Burroughs, though years before, these authors wrote existential dramas that happened to take place in Mexico but were more interested in the drama itself than the setting. In *Queer*, the country of the tricolor flag is a remote, nebulous entity. When it does show up, its worst, vilest aspects are shown. Like *The Power and the Glory*, *Queer* can seem anti-Mexican, and to a certain degree it is. Unlike Kerouac's writing on Mexico, where the descriptions of sordidness are tempered by a strong dose of compassion, never delivered in a fit of rage, *Queer* is full of scorn and resentment toward Mexico. There is never any empathy, much less admiration or recognition of any virtues, as in the correspondence of those years. But Burroughs was not devastated by Mexico: despite the country's Kafkaesque and uncivilized disposition, he never stopped liking it, except when it came to Joan's death, the great unmentionable in the novel. In Greene's work there is hatred toward Mexico; in Burroughs's, merely annoyance.

MAN OF LETTERS

It wasn't all drama for Burroughs. While he was awaiting the final verdict of the Mexican judges, writing and shooting up, supposedly to get his mind off Marker, once in a while he also had a drink at the Bounty or the Ku Ku and saw his gringo pals, slept with Angelo, or took in a bullfight or cockfight, thrilled by the violence in them: "Been seeing a lot of bullfights. Good kicks. Going to a cockfight this evening. I like my spectacles brutal, bloody and degrading" (Harris, *The Letters of William S. Burroughs*, 109).

Unlike Kerouac or D. H. Lawrence, Burroughs liked the bullfights, which he would go to with Louis Carpio and other pals, wearing a straw hat to keep the odd hurled bottle from cracking open his head. Sometimes he'd also watch the spectacle on TV.

In late March 1952, Burroughs got some good news from his adept literary agent, Ginsberg: Ace Books, a publisher where Carl Solomon (Allen's former roommate at Bellevue) worked and whose director, A. A. Wyn, was a relative, had accepted *Junky* for publication as a paperback. Ginsberg had also obtained an $850 advance for Burroughs. The Ugly Spirit was cashing in. Burroughs got the advance and offered 10 percent to Ginsberg, to whom he felt profoundly grateful: "You really are a sweetheart. I could kiss you on both cheeks. We should get used to calling each other sweetheart" (ibid., 111).

Junky would be published in the same volume with the story "Narcotic Agent" by a former agent for the Federal Bureau of Narcotics named Maurice Helbrant. The book was published in 1953 after Burroughs had already left

Mexico, and he signed it under the pseudonym William Lee, using his mother's surname. After a year on the market, 113,170 copies were sold, not a bad showing. But as a literary author, Burroughs went unnoticed. There were no reviews of the book in newspapers or magazines, no critics' articles. His name was never mentioned by anyone on the literary scene.

The boost provided by the acceptance of *Junky* for publication was some compensation for his state of mind. The fact that his first book had been published while he was writing a second granted him an identity he had never had: he was a writer now. In a letter to Kerouac, referring to some friends at Mexico City College who had traveled to Alaska to work, he commented, "Thank God I am a man of letters and don't have to expose myself to the inclemencies of near Arctic conditions" (ibid., 114).

THE RETURN OF JACK

One morning in April 1952, Neal Cassady was driving his '50 Chevy down the highway from San Francisco to Arizona. In the rear, ensconced as best as they were able on a seatless floor, were his wife Carolyn and their two kids; in the front, at his side, sat Jack Kerouac. The Cassadys were giving the author of *On the Road* a ride to Nogales. The relationship between the two legendary friends was at an ebb; they'd gotten tired of each other. So Jack decided to grab his backpack, leave Neal's house, cross the border, and travel by bus to Mexico City to meet up with Burroughs.

Having just crossed the border, Kerouac felt as if he had "sneaked out of school when you told the teacher you were sick and she told you you could go home at 2 o'clock in the afternoon." Along the way, Jack met Enrique, a young man from Veracruz, with whom he smoked opium and marijuana in the Sonora desert. Arriving in Mexico City, Enrique invited the Beat writer to Veracruz, promising him chicks and somewhere to write, but Kerouac declined: "I never saw him after Mexico City because I had no money absolutely and I had to stay on William Seward Burroughs' couch. And Burroughs didn't want Enrique around: 'You shouldn't hang around with these Mexicans, they're all a bunch of con men'" (Kerouac, *Lonesome Traveler*, 37).

A year before his arrival in Mexico, Jack had written—in three weeks, on a continuous roll of paper—the manuscript for *On the Road*. All the publishers to whom he pitched the novel, including Ace Books, declined to publish it. Some suggested changes, others turned him down flat. Because Kerouac was unwilling to remove a single comma from the original manuscript, *On the Road* languished on a dusty shelf in his room for six years before finally being published in 1957.

In the supreme novel of the Beat Generation, Burroughs, who had read the manuscript, appeared under the alias of Old Bull Balloon (which Kerouac had used in his previous novel, *The Town and the City*), a moniker he was not at all pleased with: "I am not entirely happy about appearing under the name of Old Bull Balloon. I cannot but feel that the epithet Bull contains an uncomplimentary reference, and I am by no means old. You'll be equipping me with white hair next book" (Harris, *The Letters of William S. Burroughs*, 108).

Kerouac paid him no mind and when the definitive version of his legendary and most important book came out, William Seward Burroughs was called Old Bull Lee.

Upon arriving in Mexico, the practically broke Kerouac accompanied Burroughs to the bullfights, only to despise them. He had never liked them. The ritual struck him as cruel and bloody. He also visited the pre-Hispanic ruins around Mexico City. Jack had a couple of brief affairs: with an American woman and a Mexican prostitute. At 210-5

Orizaba, he began to write a sui generis novel: *Dr. Sax*, a work of fantasy—he subtitled it *Faust Part III*—whose chief character was inspired by Burroughs.

As Burroughs took great care not to arouse suspicion over his vices, which might lead to undesirable consequences with the police, he did not allow Jack to smoke marijuana whenever he felt like it and closed doors and windows to keep the smell of the herb from reaching the nostrils of his gossipy, loose-lipped neighbors. So the prophet of the beatniks chose to lock himself in the bathroom, sit on the toilet, light his joints, shoot up an ampoule of morphine, and there write his work of fantasy. In under two months he had finished 250 pages of *Dr. Sax*. At the end of the manuscript, he wrote, "Written in Mexico Tenochtitlan, 1952, Ancient Capital of Azteca." A day before he finished the book, incidentally, he went to a Mexico City movie house to see *The Wizard of Oz*, a film that somehow inspired him to conclude the work.

This time, however, Burroughs and Kerouac did not get along and things got tense between them. Burroughs found Kerouac inconsiderate and selfish:

> I was really surprised and shocked by Jack's behavior. For example, I had asked him to keep the grass—I had

bought it—out of the apartment in case of a shake, except what he was using. . . . I pointed out to him that: 1) I was out on bail and in trouble already; 2) It was my apartment; 3) I had a habit. So what does he do? He wants Dave to bring him the bag so he can hide it somewhere without telling me. Dave told me about this plan and I put a stop to it.

That was only one of many such incidents showing a complete lack of any consideration. . . . I am not a difficult person to get along with, and I am willing to make every allowance for eccentricities, but I simply cannot get along with Jack. . . . He needs analysis. He's so paranoid he thinks everyone else is plotting to take advantage of him so he has to act first in self-defense. For example, when we were out of money and food, I could always rely on him to eat all the food there was if he got the chance. If there were two rolls left, he would always eat both of them. Once he flew into a rage because I had eaten my half of the remaining butter. If anyone asks him to do his part or to share on an equal basis, he thinks they are taking advantage of him. This is insane. (Ibid., 136)

As if that weren't enough, Jack ran out of money within a week of his arrival in Mexico, so he had to borrow a certain amount from Burroughs, which he promised to return as soon as he got back to the United States. He never did it, which angered Burroughs even more. After several months, not even a postcard had arrived.

A little while before Kerouac left Mexico, in July, Neal Cassady drove his Chevy to his old pal's rescue. After a chilly farewell, the two mythical friends got in the car and drove like hell to San Francisco. Along the way, Neal wanted to teach Jack to drive—he had never learned. "All I know how to drive is my typewriter," he might have told his fast-moving friend.

AN OVERCOAT THIEF IN MEXICO

No sooner had Kerouac left than another visitor arrived: Bill Garver, Burroughs's old New York junkie partner, the overcoat thief, who wanted to move in with him. When Burroughs went to the airport to get him, Garver's pants were stained with blood, as he'd used a safety pin to shoot up during the flight. Garver, who had inherited a certain sum of money, had the idea of residing in Mexico. He was tall and square, with his graying hair combed back, and he could not live without stealing or shooting up. Although quiet and composed, he was prone to abrupt, unforeseen outbursts.

One day, Bernabé Jurado told Burroughs that he had an ounce of something that looked like heroin, and as he himself only used cocaine, he was interested in selling it. Burroughs told Garver about Jurado's offer and the pair went over to his office. Once there the two tasters injected the grayish substance into the veins of their arms before the indifferent gaze of Jurado's staff. Burroughs confirmed that it was indeed heroin, but he didn't like it. He felt it was impure. Garver, who had taken Nembutal earlier, did like it and bought the whole ounce from Jurado. The next day at eleven in the morning, Garver went and sat down next to the bed of a fast-asleep Burroughs.

"You just going to lie there on your bed with all these shipments coming in?" Garver said to him.

"Shipments of what?" Burroughs responded in annoyance.

"Good, pure M," said Garver, uncovering Burroughs, and got into bed with him, fully clothed.

"What's the matter with you, you crazy?" said Burroughs, who noticed that his friend was distraught. He took him to his room and hid the ounce of heroin. Garver had overdosed on the drug.

A little while later, Dave Tesorero, who Burroughs was seeing again, arrived with laudanum to reduce the effects.

They put a belt around Garver's neck and at last he calmed down. Predicting that his friend would not wake up again, Burroughs suggested that Tesorero look for his wallet, which contained sixty dollars, and hold on to it before the police arrived, since they would surely pocket the money. They looked for it in his jacket, in his pants pockets, and in his suitcases but came up with nothing.

The next day, Garver got up as if nothing had happened, looking fine and fully recovered. He got dressed and, raising his mattress, took out a wallet full of bills, glad that he'd stashed it away.

Burroughs was getting bored with Garver, despite the fact that he put clips of Orozco paintings on the walls of his room, had read H. G. Wells's *A Short History of the World* dozens of times, and was a scholar of the life and work of Alexander the Great, or perhaps because of these things. In 1955, Jack Kerouac visited Garver and wrote *Mexico City Blues* and *Tristessa*. A little before the old junkie passed, Kerouac went back to visit him, this time with Ginsberg and the Orlovsky brothers.

During that period, Burroughs tried peyote for the first time in his life. The cactus rejected Burroughs, who went through a cruel and unpleasant experience under its influence:

I have never been so painfully sick. That peyote came up solid out of my stomach like a ball of hair. I thought I'd never get it out. I suffered excruciating spasms of the asposegus or whatever you call it, and it took me ten minutes to get that peyote out of my stomach and clogged my throat all the way up like I was a tube of toothpaste. (Ibid., 130)

Despite the benign impact of opium and marijuana on Burroughs, peyote never let him into its magic kingdom.

THE DEPARTURE

Apart from sharing his home with his two visitors, Burroughs was writing regularly in a disciplined fashion, alternately shooting up and trying to kick, anxiously and resignedly awaiting the definitive trial in his case so he could leave Mexico and head for South America, and carrying on an intense correspondence with his literary agent and confidant Allen Ginsberg, in which the issue of Joan was never once broached, even superficially. Burroughs simply didn't want to talk about the death of his wife. In just one instance was he unable to resist the urge to write to his friend, "How I miss Joan!"

When Marker returned to Mexico in September, things between them did not change. In a letter to Ginsberg, Burroughs describes the return of his prodigal lover:

Marker is back. I don't know whether I am glad or not. I guess I am. He was here 5 days before he came to see me, and I was hurt and couldn't help making somewhat of a scene. He said he values my friendship and I guess he does after his fashion. Then he says: "Why can't we just be friends without no sex?" I explained it was too much strain on me, I couldn't make it that way, but just once in a while like once or twice a month, so finally he comes around to agree to that.

Needless to say, the strain is still considerable, but since he is here I can't help but see him even if it is ruining my digestion, sleep and nerves. (Ibid., 137)

After a year of waiting in vain for his final trial, Burroughs was starting to get desperate. His old notions and feelings about Mexico now struck him as ludicrous. Mexico had turned into a nightmare: "All I want is out of this miserable cold town. . . . Three years in this town and no one I want to say goodbye to when I leave, except Marker. It seems people get stupider and more worthless every day."

Burroughs was sick and tired of the Mexicans. He wanted

to get out and never return. Even the bullfights now bored him. Even though his feelings toward Mexico were sometimes contradictory, he'd had enough.

In December, Marker went to Oklahoma and Burroughs had had it with Mexico. It seemed as if his case would never be resolved. He could no longer tolerate the situation. Against this backdrop, something not terribly unusual happened to Bernabé Jurado. He was driving around contentedly in his Cadillac when he felt something hit his rear fender. Never the slowpoke, he stopped the super-vehicle, got out, saw the guilty party in front of him, a sixteen-year-old, pulled a gun out of his jacket, and fired a couple of times at the leg of the hapless youth, who collapsed right in the street. The ambulance arrived and took the boy to the hospital. It seemed he would recover, but a few days later he died suddenly of tetanus. Jurado could not believe it. He'd fired without meaning to kill the kid. Bernabé wanted no trouble. He packed what he could and fled to Brazil.

Hearing of these incidents, Burroughs went to the office of Jurado, whose staff, emboldened by the absence of their boss, asked him for money so as to keep litigating his case, or so they said. Burroughs wasn't going to give them a centavo. In his head now there remained room for only one idea: to emulate his Mexican lawyer and get far away from the country, even if it meant breaking the law and losing the two thousand dollars bail that the authorities had set at the trials.

In mid-December, Burroughs filled some suitcases with his belongings, said good-bye to Bill Garver, and, hearing that a well-known American—Tex Riddle, the Trotskyist, a sort of internationalist communist—was going to travel by car to the U.S. border, made arrangements to ride with him. A few days before he left Mexico, Kerouac (with whom he had made amends) and Cassady arrived at 210-5 Orizaba. Before Burroughs departed, Cassady went back to the United States and Kerouac moved in with Garver. After a long, uneventful car trip in which Tex suggested that Burroughs rob a bank and flee to Bolivia with the dough, Burroughs crossed the border without any difficulty. Arriving in the United States, he headed for his parents' home in Palm Beach, Florida, to spend Christmas with Billy, his father Mortimer, and his mother Laura. Mexico was behind him now.

Garver died at 210-5 Orizaba in 1957. He had never stopped shooting up or stealing.

THE PARTING SHOT

In Florida, Burroughs spent a few weeks with Billy. But, as
he held on to his plans to go to South America, he said good-
bye to his son in mid-January, leaving Billy with Mortimer
and Laura again, and traveled to Panama. The ambiguity
he now felt toward Mexico was apparent in a letter he wrote
to Ginsberg from Florida on December 23, 1952:

> My income has survived the treachery and fall of Jurado.
> I lost only the bond money. I should never have expected
> to recover one peso of the money knowing the Mexicans
> as I do. I have a few bones to pick with that loud-mouthed
> bum if I ever see him again.
>
> I don't like it here. I don't dislike it. I feel that my
> home is south of the Río Grande. Mexico City is more
> home to me than any other place, but that is out for a year
> or so. (Ibid., 143)

More than to find a farm and become independent, his
objective in traveling to the southern continent was to try
yagé. The plant offered Burroughs a kind of salvation; it
seemed capable of anything except leaving him as he was before he took it. His quest was something like an act of faith,
a ritual. Bill Garver, after having his hemorrhoids treated
in a hospital, joined Burroughs in Panama but left immedi-

ately when he realized it was easier to get drugs in Mexico. Burroughs was glad to see Garver go. He couldn't take him anymore, and their plans to do something together in Panama were scrapped. Garver was insufferable; he went so far as to say bad things about Joan.

Burroughs arrived in Bogotá at the end of the month. There he got in touch with an American botanist specializing in psychoactive plants, Richard Evans Schultes, who recommended he go to the Putumayo River, located where Colombia borders Peru and Ecuador. After a long and rough journey, Burroughs arrived in Puerto Assís, where he was arrested for having an expired visa (actually, the date had been misstamped) and contracted malaria. Running a high temperature, he had to get back to Bogotá and straighten out his papers. When that was taken care of, Schultes proposed that Burroughs join a multinational expedition with two Englishmen from the Imperial Mycological Institute, three Swedish photographers who were going to catch an anaconda, five Colombian helpers, and Schultes himself, all bound for the Putumayo.

In Mocoa, Burroughs visited a *brujo*'s cabin and tried *yagé* for the first time. It was terrible: a four-hour nightmare of nonstop vomiting. A bad trip. It seemed that the *brujo* had deliberately slipped him an altered dose. Burroughs returned to Bogotá by plane and from there traveled to Lima: "Lima also has an extensive Chinatown, good restaurants, pleasant climate, the cheapest living I hit in SA . . . but I still like Mexico better."

He wrote this message to Ginsberg on May 12. In Lima, Burroughs slept with young Peruvians who cost him very little, wrote in longhand (not having a typewriter), fell ill with neuritis, read Zen texts, and at the beginning of June went to Pullcalpa, a town in the Amazon jungle where he again tried *yagé*, now in conveniently prepared doses. He took it five times. The experience was completely different from the first time.

> It is not like weed nor anything else I have ever experienced. I am now prepared to believe the brujos do have secrets. . . . The effect can not be put into words. . . .
>
> Yagé . . . is the drug that really does what the others are supposed to do.
>
> I experienced first a complete feeling of serene wisdom so that I was quite content to sit there indefinitely. What followed was indescribable. It was like possession by a blue spirit (I would paint it if I could paint). Blue purple . . .
>
> Yes, yagé is the final kick and you are not the same after you have taken it. (Ibid., 171, 180, 184)

After the long-awaited *yagé* trip, Burroughs felt like someone else, though actually he went on feeling the same as ever, or worse. The Ugly Spirit would never leave him alone again. His Mexican experiences had the effect of making him idealize *yagé* and its consequences. Burroughs required a significant, quasi-sacred quest to fill the vacuum left by Joan's death. But he hadn't touched bottom yet.

At the beginning of August, after a three-month stay in Peru, Burroughs traveled to Mexico City. He entered the country without any trouble and went looking for Marker but didn't find him; Marker had apparently gone to Guatemala to work as a tour guide. Since Burroughs's departure from Mexico in December, he had sent Marker at least ten letters from Florida without receiving any reply.

Back in Mexico City, he received a copy of *Junky* at last. He was pleased to see his first book published. Taking advantage of his brief stay in the city, Burroughs decided to visit Joan's grave at the American Cemetery, something he'd never done before. It was raining that day. Burroughs entered the cemetery and went looking for the grave of the woman with whom he'd experienced so much. He didn't even know where it was. Hard as he tried, he couldn't find it. As the rain pelted him, he quite probably shed a few tears. The rain never let up after he left the cemetery.

In mid-August, Burroughs left Mexico, never to return. The Ugly Spirit, sprung from Mexican soil, stuck with him ever since.

A CONTRIBUTION FROM MEXICO TO THE WORLD

Burroughs came to Mexico more to escape the United States than to visit its southern neighbor. Mexico struck him as grotesque, sordid, and malodorous, but he liked it. In the three years that he lived in Mexico City, his feelings toward the Mexicans were varied and contradictory. He would go from admiration and idealization of their customs and ways of life to hatred and harsh condemnation of the same things. That said, he never stopped liking Mexico. Something about it appealed to him. Perhaps it was that odd cultural intermingling, an ill-matched combination of tradition and modern spirit that makes this country as eager to modernize as it is unable to do so, giving rise to a semisavage, informal behavior in its social relations that sets it apart from the "civility" of first-world countries, whose savagery, though perhaps greater, reveals itself less directly. Mexico seemed less hypocritical than other countries to Burroughs.

Burroughs lived elusively in Mexico. He never had any interest in its culture (except, to some degree, its pre-Hispanic heritage), its politics, history, art, writers, painters, monuments. Nor did he appreciate its popular culture (except for certain pre-Hispanic echoes such as Day of the Dead), cinema, nightlife, mambos, cha-cha-chas, *charros*, mariachis, tent shows, or festivals. Burroughs's connections to Mexico derived from his then-current interests: a far-fetched idea of buying land, scoring drugs, and writing. Thus he related to people like Bernabé Jurado and Dave Tesorero (who died in 1954) and had more interest in the life of Lola la Chata than that of Alfonso Reyes or Martín Luis Guzmán, who he'd never even heard of. Whatever social life he had was with Americans, with whom he drank, ate, made love, and went to bullfights.

His passage through Mexico was crucial. In a sense, it was here that his visionary and literary vocation was born. Mexico was the scenario chosen by the gods to reveal his fate to him. It was on Mexican soil that he was entrusted with the mission of reading the world in an appallingly original manner, of seeing it through unaccustomed eyes, of verifying human deviance from an unprecedented flank. The Ugly Spirit, the emissary that forced this mission upon him, emerged from Mexico's magical magma, its volcanic energy, its witchcraft. Some Nahualic force must have chosen William S. Burroughs as a vehicle for expressing his shamanic images to mankind. The story is written: Burroughs went to Mexico to be possessed by the puffs of breath of a malicious, feisty, prophetic urchin who endowed him with the gift of *seeing*. What ensued was one of the greatest contributions to the world—or underworld—that ever sprang from Mexican soil. For that reason, William S. Burroughs's readers are eternally grateful to the most magical hybrid of a country in existence. ¡Viva México!

A NOTE ON SOURCES

Various sources were consulted in the writing of this book: books, interviews, letters, newspapers, and so on. Books on the life of William S. Burroughs before and during his stay in Mexico include Ted Morgan, *Literary Outlaw* (New York: Avon Books, 1990); Barry Gifford and Lawrence Lee, *Jack's Book* (New York: St. Martin's Press, 1994); and Carolyn Cassady, *Off the Road* (New York: William Morrow and Company, 1990), the source of the quotation from Ginsberg's letter to the author after Joan's death.

The following people were interviewed about the life of William S. Burroughs in Mexico: Doña Marina, tenant of the building at 210 Orizaba, Roma district; Manuel Mejía, former employee of the building at 122 Monterrey, Roma district; Lupita Peñaloza, cousin of Juanita Peñaloza, administrator of the building at 122 Monterrey; John Paddock, former student at Mexico City College; Miguel López Sandoval, a lawyer who knew Bernabé Jurado; María del Carmen Juárez, former employee at Mexico City Women's Prison who knew Lola la Chata; John Healy, friend of William S. Burroughs in Mexico (by James Grauerholz); and Burroughs himself.

These newspapers were consulted: *Excélsior*, *El Nacional*, *Novedades*, and *La Prensa*, from which some of the photographs published here were taken.

For accounts by Lewis Marker, Eddie Woods, Hal Chase, Kells Elvins, and Marianne Wolf, the archives of Ted Morgan were consulted; quotations by Kells Elvins and Marianne Wolf are from this source.

Books by Jack Kerouac that were consulted are *On the Road* (New York: Penguin Group, 1976), *Tristessa* (New York: Penguin Group, 1992), *Lonesome Traveler* (New York: Grove Press, 1988), and *Dr. Sax* (New York: Grove Press, 2007).

Quotations from William S. Burroughs's correspondence were taken from *The Letters of William S. Burroughs, 1945–1959*, ed. Oliver Harris (New York: Viking, 1993). The works of William S. Burroughs that were consulted and quoted include *Junky* (New York: Penguin Books, 1977); *Queer* (New York: Penguin Books, 1985); with Allen Ginsberg, *The Yage Letters Redux* (San Francisco: City Lights Books, 2006); and by William S. Burroughs Jr., *Speed/Kentucky Ham* (New York: Overlook Press, 1993).

The archives of Columbia University were consulted for correspondence between Kerouac and Ginsberg.

An account of Mexico City of the period was taken from Salvador Novo, *La vida de México en el período presidencial de Miguel Alemán* (Mexico City: Empresas Editoriales, 1967). The bulletins of Mexico City College were also used.

JORGE GARCÍA-ROBLES

is a Mexican novelist, critic, and translator; he is considered the leading authority on the Beats in Mexico. He translated Jack Kerouac's *Lonesome Traveler*, *Tristessa*, *Mexico City Blues*, and "Cerrada Medellín Blues" and William S. Burroughs's *The Yage Letters* into Spanish.

DANIEL C. SCHECHTER

is an American writer and translator now living in the Netherlands. He has translated articles for the Mexican publications *Artes de México* and *Escala* and has contributed to many Lonely Planet guidebooks.